I hope
your penis
shrivels up!

**Books by the same author include:**

*The Medicine Men* (1975)
*Paper Doctors* (1976)
*Everything You Want to Know About Ageing* (1976)
*Stress Control* (1978)
*The Home Pharmacy* (1980)
*Aspirin or Ambulance* (1980)
*Face Values* (1981)
*Guilt* (1982)
*The Good Medicine Guide* (1982)
*Stress and Your Stomach* (1983)
*Bodypower* (1983)
*Thomas Winsden's Cricketing Almanack* (1983)
*A Guide to Child Health* (1984)
*An A to Z of Women's Problems* (1984)
*Bodysense* (1984)
*Taking Care of Your Skin* (1984)
*Diary of a Cricket Lover* (1984)
*Life Without Tranquillisers* (1985)
*High Blood Pressure* (1985)
*Diabetes* (1985)
*Arthritis* (1985)
*Eczema and Dermatitis* (1985)
*The Story of Medicine* (1985)
*Natural Pain Control* (1986)
*Mindpower* (1986)
*Addicts and Addictions* (1986)
*Dr Vernon Coleman's Guide to Alternative Medicine* (1988)
*Stress Management Techniques* (1988)
*Overcoming Stress* (1988)
*Know Yourself* (1988)
*The Health Scandal* (1988)
*The 20 Minute Health Check* (1989)
*Sex for Everyone* (1989)
*Mind Over Body* (1989)
*Eat Green Lose Weight* (1990)
*Toxic Stress* (1991)
*Why Animal Experiments Must Stop* (1991)
*The Drugs Myth* (1992)
*Arthritis* (1993)
*Backache* (1993)
*Stress and Relaxation* (1993)
*Complete Guide to Good Sex* (1993)
*Why Doctors Do More Harm Than Good* (1993)
*Betrayal of Trust* (1994)

*Know Your Drugs* (1994)
*Food for Thought* (1994)
*The Traditional Home Doctor* (1994)

Novels
*The Village Cricket Tour* (1990)
*The Bilbury Chronicles* (1992)
*Bilbury Grange* (1993)
*Mrs Caldicot's Cabbage War* (1993)
*The Man Who Inherited a Golf Club* (1993)
*The Bilbury Revels* (1994)
*Deadline* (1994)

Writing as Edward Vernon
*Practice Makes Perfect* (novel, 1977)
*Practise What You Preach* (novel, 1978)
*Getting into Practice* (novel, 1979)
*Aphrodisiacs—An Owner's Manual* (1983)
*The Complete Guide to Life* (1984)

As Marc Charbonnier
*Tunnel* (novel, 1980)

With Dr Alan C. Turin
*No More Headaches* (1981)

With Alice
*Alice's Diary* (1989)
*Alice's Adventures* (1992)

# I hope your penis shrivels up!

...and other
helpful advice

Philosophy, sex and life –
answers to problems of
every kind

# Vernon Coleman

European
Medical
Journal

# A note to readers

This book is not intended as an alternative to personal, professional medical advice. The reader should consult a physician in all matters relating to health, and particularly in respect of any symptoms which may require diagnosis or medical attention.

While the advice and information are believed to be accurate at the time of going to press, neither the author nor the publisher can accept any legal responsibility or liability for any errors or omissions that may be made.

Remember: sex can cause pregnancy and spread diseases. Take precautions.

ALL ROYALTIES AND PROCEEDS FROM THE SALE OF THIS BOOK GO TO HELP THE CAMPAIGN AGAINST ANIMAL EXPERIMENTS

First published in the United Kingdom by the European Medical Journal, Lynmouth, Devon, EX35 6EE, England

ISBN   1 898947 05 8

A catalogue record for this book is available from the British Library

Printed and bound in England by Biddles Ltd., Guildford and King's Lynn

# Dedication

To Vicky, whose laughter is inspiration

## Quotes from this book

'The instant they become teenagers, kids suffer a hormonal explosion which turns them into psychotic, spotty, arrogant, self centred, repulsive know it alls.'

'If breasts got bigger when handled, 97% of teenage girls would be size 38DD.'

'Straight pubic hair isn't unusual—and certainly isn't kinky.'

'It can take hours for a sperm to swim and meet an egg—the girl in the supermarket could be getting pregnant while she slips your breadsticks into your bag.'

'Some men are sensible enough to realise that the size of a woman's breasts is not as important as her personality, sense of humour, generosity of spirit and capacity for love.'

'Reasonable behaviour would have been to throw your food at the wall and walk out.'

'It is considered polite for a man who has been making love in the missionary position to clamber off his partner before starting to snore.'

'Lots of women secretly hate, despise and resent their own children.'

'You can't be a bit of a virgin any more than you can be a bit dead.'

'A woman who accepts £5 for sex is a prostitute just as much as a woman who accepts £1,000. She's just not as good at it.'

'The only real question is whether your wife will stab you repeatedly with a sharp kitchen knife or bludgeon you to death with a blunt object.'

'No human activity is without risk. A man I know once knelt down to pray in church and impaled his knee upon a protruding nail.'

'Slimmers should remember the Tenth Commandment: Thou shalt not covet thy neighbour's ass.'

'For procreation it doesn't matter a toss whether a woman has an orgasm. Please send complaints to the manufacturer. He is open on Sundays.'

'Only when you've found something you're prepared to die for will you really know what life is all about.'

'People who behave the way your boss does are usually conscious of the fact that their shoe size is greater than their IQ.'

•He sounds the sort of person who starts the day with a raw liver sandwich, washes it down with a quart of rubbing alcohol and prepares himself for the day's work by watching old newsreel footage of Adolf Hitler practising the Berchtes-gaden strut for his performances at the Berlin Odeon.'

•Has it occurred to you that the two lumps on your girl friend's chest are actually part of her body?'

•Isn't it odd how everyone who can recall a previous existence always claims to have been someone romantic and fascinating?'

•The real tragedy is that millions of people are dead at twenty. They get carried on through life like driftwood, never taking control of their own destiny.'

•'Might have been' is the saddest phrase I know.'

•When you are old your regrets will tell you more about yourself than your accomplishments.'

•You'll know he really loves you when he tells you he loves you *after* you've had sex.'

•You should start worrying when your husband deliberately averts his eyes when tempted by a flash of creamy white high or a provocative hint of awe inspiring cleavage.'

•The main troubled with the world is that someone put the grownups in charge.'

•The arrival of tights marked the end of modern civilisation.'

•I can sum up everything I wish to say to you in just two words. The second word is 'off'.'

•Your husband is a boil waiting to burst.'

•I just hope your boyfriend has the strength to tell you to piss off out of his life.'

•I hope you give birth to two snivelling children who go to university, grow to despise you and make you realise, in old age, that your entire life has been a waste.'

•May your orgasms always be elusive and your friends always faithless.'

•I am told that having a spittoon in the bedroom is considered rather common in some circles.'

•Most parents lose any vestiges of hope when their ungrateful children finally turn into whining teenagers.'

•When your children finally metamorphose into young adults you can get your own back by encouraging them to marry and to have children of their own.'

'An army of pseudo intellectual vigilantes, armed with suspicion and wagging fingers, now patrols every aspect of twentieth century life. In the world in which these mind control fascists would have us live, jokes and lingerie would be outlawed.'

'Once I was told I was being sacked because I made people think.'

'You could start a serious and meaningful relationship with a ferret. Male ferrets have erections which last up to eight hours.'

'If you've been brought up to think of it as normal for overweight accountants to barbecue sausages in the nude then nudism probably does seem perfectly natural. The fact is, however, that most of like to have somewhere to keep our handkerchiefs.'

'I would suggest that you buy a plastic blow up doll but even plastic blow up dolls have standards.'

'May the zip on your fly always catch on your tender bits.'

'It must be quite fun to be able to listen to your husband's wild and unbridled fantasies about that pompous woman in tweeds who always talks as though she has got her mouth full and walks as though she got a prize winning courgette stuck up her bum.'

• Hannibal was Commander in Chief of the Carthaginian army at the age of 26—in charge of 40,000 troops and 38 elephants—so running a florist's shop doesn't seem an entirely unreasonable ambition.'

• Your boyfriend sounds as if he is what he has—a large male organ.'

• Life isn't fair or predictable. You have to take it by the scruff of the neck.'

• The load bearing capacity of the erect human penis is around 5 to 6 pounds, but this is generally regarded as a theoretical capacity rather than a practical capability.'

## INTRODUCTION

This book doesn't really need an introduction. But I know that some people are old fashioned about this sort of thing, and like everything to be done properly, so this is just to introduce *I Hope Your Penis Shrivels Up* to you. Now that you have both been formally introduced to one another I hope you thoroughly enjoy each other's company. Be gentle with one another and please feel free to blame me if it doesn't work out.

Vernon Coleman, Devon 1994

## PREFACE

This book doesn't really need a Preface either but since it has a Note, a Dedication, a Forword and an Introduction, I thought it ought to have a Preface as well.

Vernon Coleman, still in Devon, still 1994

# I hope your penis shrivels up!

## ...and other helpful advice

......................................................

### FOURTEEN

I am 14 and I want to divorce my parents because they don't understand me. I want to go and live with my grandparents who are much kinder to me. My parents make me do homework but my gran lets me watch TV and always gives me burgers.

Your parents have a duty to feed you and clothe you. They do not have a duty to understand you. Anyone who claims to understand a teenager is almost certainly psychologically unbalanced.

At the age of 12 years, 364 days 23 hours and 59 minutes most children are quite nice. They ask a lot of bloody stupid questions and make endless messes but they can be tolerably cute.

One second later, as they become teenagers, kids suffer a hormonal explosion which instantly turns them into psychotic, spotty, arrogant, self centred, repulsive know it alls. Teenagers suffer from a number of delusions. They think that they have been endowed with the wisdom of the world. They think they are interesting, charming and bright and imbued with fascinating, mature opinions. They think that the world revolves around their absurd and irrelevant needs and they think that all adults are not only stupid but are put on this earth to attend to their every need.

This paper thin sense of delusion, wisdom and self regard stays with teenagers until they reach the age of 19 years, 364 days, 23 hours and 59 seconds. Then, quite suddenly, they stop being teenagers, become dull witted adults and realise that they don't know a bloody thing about anything.

What I suspect you mean is that your grandparents are prepared to indulge your whims and fancies and listen to your whingeing without wincing.

If you really want to try living with your grandparents I suggest that you offer to cut the lawn, do the shopping and tidy up your bedroom. Your parents will have to be hospitalised for a month and this will give you the opportunity to try life with gran.

........................................................................

## TELEPHONE SEX

My boyfriend is a salesman and has to spend a lot of time away from home. A few months ago we both saw a film in which the two lead characters talked dirty to each other on the telephone. We now do this regularly two or three times a week and both find it a very satisfying way to get rid of our sexual frustrations. Do you think it can do any harm?

No. You won't go blind or even short sighted. And you won't grow hair on the palms of your hands. But I do have one warning for you. Make sure that it's your boyfriend on the phone before you go into your telephone routine. A friend of mine (whose husband was working away from home) used to have telephone sex every Wednesday at 10.00 pm. One evening the phone went as usual and she picked it up and went straight into action.

'I'm wearing my sexy black undies,' she began breathlessly. 'I'm taking my bra off and fondling my breasts. What are you doing?' 'I was ringing to tell you that my husband would be round tomorrow to repair your central heating boiler,' said a rather cold, feminine voice. 'But it doesn't sound to me as though you need any central heating and even if you do it certainly won't be my husband coming to repair your boiler.'

My friend says that this was terrible for three reasons. First, she had been waiting two weeks for the boiler to be repaired. Second, when her husband did ring she was in such a state that she was is no condition to talk sexy. And third, she later discovered that the boiler repairer's son was in the same class as her own at the local school. 'I could never look that woman in the face,' she told me. 'And I was terribly relieved when they left the area.'

## BREAST MASSAGE

Can I change the shape and increase the size of my breasts with massage?

No. If breasts got bigger when handled 97% of teenage girls would be size 38DD. The only part of the human body which noticeably changes size and shape with massage is exclusively male.

## PUBERTY

At what age is it normal for a girl to reach puberty?

Eleven or twelve. About a hundred years ago girls reached puberty at the age of 16. By 1950 it had dropped to thirteen. Today it isn't uncommon for girls to start showing signs of womanhood (developing breasts, strands of pubic hair etc.) at ten. A diet that contains more fatty food than it used to is probably responsible.

### SHOUTING OUT

When my husband and I make love I often shout out loud
and make a lot of other noises. We have been invited to
stay with friends for the New Year but I'm a bit worried. Is
there anything I can do to make sure that I don't make any
embarrassing noises while we're there? (There will be quite
a lot of other people staying there at the same time).

Take a good book with you and ask your hostess for
single beds and two hot water bottles.

### STRAIGHT, NOT KINKY

My pubic hair is straight. I didn't realise this was odd until
I started to go into the showers at school. Is it anything to
worry about? One of the other girls says it means I must
be odd in some way.

No. Straight pubic hair is unusual. But it isn't dangerous.
And it certainly isn't kinky.

### JUST LOOKING

My husband says he loves me but I often catch him looking
at other women. Do you think this means that I am failing
to satisfy him in some way? What should I do about it?

You don't need to do anything. All normal, healthy men
look at other women. You should start worrying when
he stops looking: that means he's got something to hide,
feels guilty and is behaving unnaturally in order to try to
put you off the scent. Men are stupid like that.

### TEAM DREAM

Last night I dreamt that I made love to the other ten players in my husband's football team while he simply stood and watched. I have had this dream several times since I have been pregnant. Is this anything I should be worried about? (I feel rather guilty about it because I seem to enjoy myself in the dream).

I'm tempted to ask if your husband is the goal-keeper because it certainly sounds as if he doesn't score very often. But I won't. I bet you've been avoiding sex because your doctor has warned you that sex could damage your pregnancy (though sex isn't normally a threat to a healthy baby). Because you aren't allowed to have sex with your husband you're having sex with men other than your husband in your dreams. Simple—and absolutely nothing at all for you to worry about or feel guilty about. Enjoy your dream.

## BRAIN FOOD

Is it true that fish is good food for the brain? I hate fish but my mum says I should eat it because it'll make me brainy and help me pass my exams next summer.

How many fish do you know who've passed even one school examination?

## LOSING HAIR

I am a 35-year-old male. I am losing my hair. What do you recommend?

Coming to terms with being bald.

## SPERM SPEED

How long after making love does it take for the sperm to reach an egg? My first baby was conceived while my husband and I were away for the weekend and I'm curious to know when my baby started to develop.

Your pregnancy probably didn't start until you were back at work. It can take hours for a sperm to swim up into a fallopian tube and meet an egg. And it is days after that before the pregnancy really starts. In any large factory, shop or office where there are lots of women there's a good chance that one of them will be getting pregnant while she works.

It's rather nice to think that inside the girl behind the counter at your local bank millions of tiny sperm could be jostling for position. The traffic warden slipping a ticket behind your windscreen wiper could be playing hostess to a major life or death drama. The girl in the supermarket could be getting pregnant at exactly the same moment that she is slipping your bread sticks into your carrier bag.

....................................................

## BONER FIDE

Is it true that the penis has a bone in it? A friend of mine suffered a lot of pain recently while making love and had to be taken to hospital. The doctors there said that he had fractured a bone in his penis.

Unless your friend is a man in a billion the doctors were probably 'catheterising' him (medical terminology for taking the piss out of him). There is some evidence that many thousands of years ago the penis may have contained a bone to make penetration easier. And in France thirty years ago doctors produced X-ray evidence of a man with a small bone built into his penis. (Inevitably this meant that his penis never went soft. Researchers would have liked to have got close to check things out but neither the Frenchman nor the horde of lovely young things who constantly surrounded him would let them anywhere near his valuable organ.) I think it is more likely that your friend ruptured a blood vessel or twisted a testicle.

..............................................................

## STANDING UP

Is it true that if she has a sexual experience standing up a girl can't get pregnant?

Yes. As long as she's by herself at the time. If there is a man within fifty yards she can get pregnant.

..............................................................

## EMBARRASSED CHILDREN

I am 64. I have been divorced for eleven years and have just moved in with my boyfriend. He is 67. We very much enjoy one another's company and have an active and very satisfying sex life (in fact I have done things in bed with my boyfriend which I never did with my ex-husband even though we were married for 38 years). Both my son and my daughter have said terrible things to me. My daughter lives with a man she isn't married to but although I have never criticised her for this she says that what I am doing is embarrassing her. Neither my boyfriend nor I want to get married—our feeling is that our relationship is perfect as it is and so 'if it ain't broke why fix it?'. I would appreciate your advice.

Having a partner you care about—and who cares for you—is important at any age. You are just as entitled to find love and companionship as your children. Their disapproval is, I suspect, inspired partly by selfishness and old fashioned prejudice and partly by the fact that they feel uncomfortable about the idea of their mother having a lover. You can try explaining all this to them (and pointing out that they are behaving in a very old fashioned way) or you can just hope that in time they will mature enough to accept that you have rights as a human being as well as obligations as a mother. It must be a real pain when your children still behave like children when they look like grown ups.

## HOLDING BACK

How long should a man be able to hold back before he ejaculates during sex? My girlfriend counts the 'in and out' movements and says that a man should be able to manage at least 200 'in and out' movements before he comes. I can't always manage this and if I come too soon she either accuses me of being selfish and not caring about her or else says I'm suffering from premature ejaculation. I'm beginning to find sex rather a strain—especially since my girlfriend has taken to counting the 'in and out' movements out aloud. How many movements should a man be able to make before he comes?

The phrase 'premature ejaculation' is completely subjective. If you come before your girlfriend is satisfied then in her terms you have, indeed, ejaculated prematurely. But let's put this into perspective. Around 75% of men ejaculate within two minutes of entering their partner and I doubt if many men would manage 200 'in and out' movements within that sort of time frame. I don't think you should be too hard on yourself. In fact, to be honest, I'm surprised that you can still manage to get an erection at all. Many men would find the prospect of having their performance rated so clinically rather intimidating. The ferret may be able to manage 8 hours of continuous sex but larger mammals, such as man, are usually quicker off the mark. (The male elephant takes only around 30 seconds to ejaculate and a chimpanzee manages only 10 seconds or so.) I would suggest that you talk to your girlfriend about this. Maybe she would be willing to allow you to take her to orgasm with the aid of oral sex or manual stimulation?

## SINGLE EAR RING

Is it true that if a man wears a single ear ring he is a homosexual?

Not necessarily. It could simply mean that he has lost the other ear ring.

••••••••••••••••••••••••••••••••••••••••••••••••••••••••••••••

## NOT KNOCKING

My two testicles hang at different heights. Is this normal?

Yes. The left one is usually slightly lower than the one on the right. They are designed this way to stop them knocking into one another.

••••••••••••••••••••••••••••••••••••••••••••••••••••••••••••••

## LONELY AND MISERABLE

My husband has been working away from home for several weeks and I've been a bit lonely and miserable recently. Last Saturday a girl friend, whose husband is in the forces and also working away from home, asked me to go into town with her for a drink. We dressed up a bit (short skirts, see through blouses and stockings and suspenders) and went to a pub I'd never been to before. There was a band playing there that my girlfriend wanted to listen to. I had a few drinks and because I'm not used to drinking I got quite tipsy, though I have to admit I wasn't drunk and I did know what I was doing.

My girl friend is a bit of a flirt and we got picked up by four lads; all of whom were quite a lot younger than us. When the pub closed we went back to a flat with them and carried on drinking and dancing.

I was sitting talking to two of the boys when I looked round and saw that my friend was kissing one of the lads and letting another fondle her below the waist. As I watched the one who was kissing her undid her blouse and took out her breasts and the other one pushed up her skirt and pulled down her knickers. Like me she was wearing stockings, not tights. She didn't try to stop them at all and to my amazement she started making love to the two lads at the same time. She was naked from the waist up but still had on her stockings and suspender belt. I had never seen anything like it and I found myself feeling quite turned on.

When one of the boys I was talking to started to fondle my breasts I didn't do anything to stop him and a few moments later I was kneeling beside her on the carpet making love to two boys whose names I didn't even know. We stayed the night and both made love to all four of the lads several times. One of them had a much bigger thing than anything I've ever seen before but to my surprise it didn't hurt at all; in fact I had incredible orgasms when he put it in me.

They didn't use condoms but I'm not worried because I know I can't get pregnant because I'm on the pill. I am, however, worried sick that my husband will find out though I think I'm probably safe because the pub was in a part of town that we never usually go to. Do you think I should write and tell my husband what happened?

You might not have to worry about being pregnant but you should worry about being infected. I think you'd be wise to pop along to the sexually transmitted disease clinic at your local hospital and ask them to check you out.

I don't think you should write and tell your husband. What the hell were you going to say?

*Dear John,*
*I hope you are well. The weather hasn't been very good. The grass needs cutting. I met four blokes in a pub and made love to them all. One of them had a very big penis—much bigger than yours. The garage roof is leaking and I had a cold last week.*
*Love,*
*Your wife*

You wouldn't be normal if you didn't feel guilty and apprehensive. But I'm afraid that's the price you have to pay for your night out. Neither you nor your husband have anything to gain from a burst of honesty on your part.

## I WAS A VIRGIN

I am 18 years old, I work as a painter and decorator, and until two weeks ago I was a virgin. My boss and I had been working on a job for three weeks when, on the last day, I was told to stay behind and clear up while my boss went to look at another job he had been asked to do. When I had finished clearing away the dust sheets, empty paint tins and so on the lady of the house, a married woman, asked me if I would like a cup of coffee. When I said 'yes' she asked me if I would like to take a shower while the kettle boiled. I said 'no' at first but she was quite insistent and so eventually I said 'yes'. When I got out of the shower I discovered there was no towel. I was just drying myself on my shirt when she came into the room, apologised and handed me a towel. Much to my embarrassment she didn't go away but just stood there and watched while I dried myself. After a moment or two she asked me if I'd like her to dry my back. I said it was all right, that I could manage, but she took the towel off me and started to rub me with it. I started to get sexually aroused almost immediately and it wasn't long before I had an enormous erection—the biggest and hardest I've ever had. She then kissed me and pressed herself against me. She was wearing this pink housecoat thing and while she held onto me with one hand she unfastened the buttons down the front with the other. I was quite shocked when she shrugged it off her shoulders to see that she had absolutely nothing on underneath it. She had very large breasts with absolutely huge nipples. What came next shocked me quite a lot. She knelt down in front of me and put my penis into her mouth. I tried to stop her and to warn her what was going to happen but she didn't seem to mind at all. After that she lay me down on the bed and we made love. Before I left she asked me if I would go back and do some odd jobs around the house for her. I said I would but now I'm a bit worried in case she wants to put my penis in her mouth again. Is that a normal thing for a woman to want to do? Is it safe for a man to come in a woman's mouth?

Stop worrying. Oral sex is a perfectly normal activity which is enjoyed by millions of women—though not all like their male partner to come in their mouths. (It is considered polite to ask your partner her preference and, whatever she says, to warn her just before your volcano erupts). If you want to worry I suggest that you start worrying about what to do if her husband comes home unexpectedly. Maybe you could use your odd job skills to construct a priest hole in the bedroom. I should, I suppose, remind you that sexual activity carries with it a risk of infection.

## TOO SMALL

My boyfriend says my breasts are too small. For months he has nagged at me to have an operation to make them bigger. As my Christmas present he gave me a cheque to pay for the surgery. But I don't particularly want to have the operation done (I don't think my breasts are particularly small) and I'm worried. I have heard that the operation can sometimes cause problems. What do you think?

It sounds to me as if your boyfriend was hoping to buy himself a present when he gave you a cheque for breast surgery. I know a lot of men buy their wives and girlfriends sexy underwear for Christmas (and expect them to be grateful!) but at least a black bra and suspender set is fairly harmless.

Your boyfriend deserves some sort of award for crass, thoughtless, crude, sexist cheek and I hope you bought him a one way ticket to Baghdad for Christmas. My advice is that you give him the cheque back. Tell him his need is greater than yours and suggest that he spends his cash on having either his brain or his penis enlarged. Your fears are well founded. Although plastic surgeons have been trying to eradicate small breasts for years (they even have a name for it: having small breasts is a disease called micromastia) there is a considerable amount of worrying evidence available to suggest that implants may not always be safe.

## SHAVED DOWN BELOW

My boyfriend persuaded me to let him shave off all my pubic hair by telling me that all top models are shaven down below. Now I quite like it. One practical advantage is that I can wear really brief bikini bottoms when I go swimming but I like it most because of the amazing effect it has had on our sex life. My boyfriend says I feel so different down there that it's like making love to a completely different woman. I have to admit that I have found that shaving has made the skin around my vagina very sensitive. The only snag is that I find that if I don't shave two or three times a week I get a bit bristly and it itches. Are there any dangers to having no pubic hair? If there aren't, is there any way to get rid of pubic hair permanently so that I don't have to shave?

Pubic hair isn't important like kidneys or lungs. I've never heard of anyone being rushed into hospital for an emergency pubic hair transplant. Technically there is no reason why you shouldn't have all your pubic hair removed. The only way to get rid of it permanently is to have the whole area treated by a specialist in electrolysis. This will be time consuming, expensive and possibly painful. And since you will then be permanently bald this will mean that if you want to ring the changes you'll have to be fitted for a pubic hair wig. Shaving is probably the best method of control. And you can always experiment with pretty patterns. One woman I know had her pubic hair trimmed into the shape of a heart. Another had hers cut so that she had two tiny pigtails—tied with little pink ribbons.

## TURKISH FRIGHT

Three months ago I went on holiday with a girlfriend to Turkey. We both have boyfriends in England and are planning to get married this year. We thought we would have a last fling. On our first night there I met a Turkish boy who asked me to go dancing with him. I was reluctant to leave my friend but he was very persuasive and eventually I said I would go as long as my girlfriend could come with us. He said that would be no problem because he had a friend who liked English girls. However, when the two of them turned up at our hotel my girlfriend refused to go. We had an argument and I went on my own with the two boys. We stayed at the dance for about three hours and then, when I said I wanted to go back to my hotel, the two boys drove me back. I kissed them both goodnight and although one of them tried to feel my breasts they behaved like perfect gentlemen.

The following night I went out dancing again with the two boys. My girlfriend had by this time made friends with a group of English holidaymakers so I didn't feel too bad about leaving her alone. When we got back to the hotel my girlfriend wasn't there so I invited the two boys in.

I was lying on my bed kissing and cuddling the one who had originally asked me out when the other one, who was lying alone on the other bed, started to cry. When I asked him what was the matter he said that girls never liked him as much as his friend and that everyone laughed at him because he had never made love to a girl. I felt sorry for him and kissed him and let him feel my breasts. Anyway, one thing led to another and before long we were all three naked. I was making love to the boy who said he'd never had a proper girl friend before, and his friend was taking photos of us with my polaroid camera, when my girl friend walked in. We had a very nasty scene. My girl friend called me a tart and the two boys eventually went off together. I never saw them again. When they left they took half a dozen very compromising photographs with them. My former girl friend hardly spoke to me for the rest of the holiday but although my boyfriend has asked why we fell out she hasn't said anything. I don't think she will.

However, I am worried about the photographs. I don't know the names of the two boys (and they don't know my name) but do you think I should try to get in touch with them via the hotel to buy back the pictures?

No. The chances of your fiancé accidentally bumping into a Turk who then opens his wallet and shows him photos of you performing a noble deed for a sad young man (if his story was true, then I suppose that what you did was rather a nice thing to do, though your boyfriend might not see it that way: if he was conning you then he deserves to get what he did to you) must be slight. If you try to get in touch with them, however, you may be creating some very messy problems for yourself.

I would, however, suggest that don't go back to that hotel for your honeymoon.

And do visit a sexually transmitted diseases clinic for a check up.

••••••••••••••••••••••••••••••••••••••••••••••••••••••••••••••••••

## ARMY DAYS

When I was 18 I spent three years in the army. One weekend when my platoon went on a training expedition I had to stay behind in the barracks because I had injured my leg. I was lying on my bed, reading magazines and bored out of my mind when another soldier wandered in on crutches. He had a broken ankle and he too had been left behind. He sat on my bed and we talked about this and that and suddenly I noticed that his hand was resting on my thigh. I should have made him move it but I didn't. I don't know why. I do know that to my surprise I did feel a stirring in my groin and when, a few moments later, he started stroking my leg I soon had an enormous erection. He asked me if I minded and I said I didn't and the next thing I knew his fingers were very expertly unfastening my fly. He took out my penis and then unfastened his own trousers. We then both performed what I believe are known as unnatural acts. I can still remember exactly what we did. When we had both finished he fastened up his trousers and left. I didn't see him again and I never did that again with anyone else. I am now 52 years old and I have been happily married for 27 years but for all of that time I have lived with the knowledge that I must have homosexual tendencies. Do you think I should tell my wife what I did and do you think I should have any tests to see if I contracted AIDS as a result of that experience?

The AIDS virus probably didn't even exist 34 years ago (at least, not in its present form). You don't need to worry about that. And I don't think you need to tell your wife about your isolated and perfectly normal homosexual adventure. Many young men—particularly in the forces—experiment with homosexuality. It is nothing to worry about and nothing to be ashamed of (though these days, of course, homosexual activities—particularly anal sex—are a major reason for the spread of AIDS). Even if you cannot erase this incident from your memory you can safely put it away somewhere and allow it to get dusty.

## LOSING HAIR

I am a 28-year-old man. I am losing my hair. Is there anything I can do about it? A friend of mine says that you can make hair grow back by rubbing animal fat on your head. Is this true?

Rubbing animal fat on your scalp may do some things for you (like increase your personal space on public transport in hot weather) but I'm afraid I don't think it will make your hair grow.

## A WOMANISER

I have worked for my present boss for seven years as his personal assistant/secretary. He is quite a womaniser and I have often had to lie for him when his wife has rung up wanting to speak to him. He often tells her he is working and then goes to a hotel with one of his mistresses. Last week, however, things reached a new low. On Thursday he asked me to go to his home to pretend to be his wife. He said that one of his mistresses had told him that on that evening she was going to go round to his home, confront his wife and tell her what had been going on. My boss is frightened of his wife finding out about his affairs because he knows that the alimony would cripple him. He wanted me to pretend to be his wife and to sit there while his mistress explained what a double crossing bastard he is. He said it would be easy to do because the mistress has never seen his wife. Moreover he said that his wife would be out for the whole of that evening attending a Parent Teacher meeting.

I am now very ashamed of the fact that I did what he wanted. I went to his home. I pretended to be his wife. And I listened as his mistress opened her heart. She was very dignified though I could tell that she was close to tears.

I feel disgusted with myself for doing this and I have already decided that I intend to find another job as soon as possible. I felt very sorry for the mistress because I know that my boss has lied to her many times before. He is a real bastard and he is dragging me down to his level.

Do you think I should tell his mistress and his wife the truth about him?

No. They won't thank you for telling them the truth. Leave your boss, as quickly as you can (or even quicker if possible). Without your protection maybe the women in his life will find out the truth about him. Maybe you could plant a few 'time bombs'. Slip a condom or something lace and flimsy into his jacket pocket and leave him to do some wriggling on his own.

• • • • • • • • • • • • • • • • • • • • • • • • • • • • • • • • • • • • • • • • • •

## LONELY

I am very lonely. I am 26, male and have a good, steady job though I work alone and don't come into contact with members of the public very much. I have never had a girlfriend or any 'mates' of my own sex. I live with my parents and would very much like to have a more lively social life. I would much appreciate any suggestions.

What are you interested in? What would you like to be interested in? Trains? Stamp collecting? Computers? Football? Art history? Opera? Water colour painting? Pot holing? Aikido? Underwater embroidery? There must be something you'd like to know more about. Once you've chosen a few subjects go down to the public library and ask the librarian to give you details about organisations and societies dealing with those subjects. Or if you just want to be fit join a gym or aerobics class. Once you start meeting more people, you'll find your social life will start to perk up.

························································································

## FALSE BREASTS

I am 14 years old and have very small breasts. I am so flat chested that I know boys will never want to go out with me. Can you please tell me how I can find a doctor prepared to give me false breasts.

There is still plenty of time for your breasts to develop. I don't believe that any reputable surgeon would operate on a 14-year-old girl—however flat chested. In two years time you could well have an enormous pair of home grown breasts. But try to get rid of this notion of yours that men are only interested with women with cleavage. Some men prefer women with large breasts, it is true. But some men like women with small breasts. Some men who like looking at women with huge breasts prefer loving women with very small breasts. And some men, you may be surprised to hear, are sensible enough to realise that the size of a woman's breasts is not as important as her personality, sense of humour, generosity of spirit and capacity for love.

························································································

## NOT CIRCUMCISED

I am 32 and have not yet been circumcised. I worry about this a lot. Do you think I should have it done or is it too late?

Roughly half the adult males everywhere outside Israel are uncircumcised. Why on earth do you want to be circumcised? As long as your foreskin is mobile enough to move back far enough for you be able to clean under it thoroughly there is no need for you to have your foreskin removed unless, for some bizarre reason, it is essential that the people with whom you shower be falsely persuaded that you are Jewish.

## DEAD ANIMALS

I am 16. I do not like the idea of eating dead animals but I want to be a body builder and I have been told that without eating meat I will not get big. Indeed, I have been warned that it is not safe for me to train in the gym if I eat a vegetarian diet. Is this true?

No. It is not true. It is bullshit. Talking of bulls, bulls don't eat meat. Elephants don't eat meat. Baboons don't eat meat. They all get much bigger than you'll ever want to be. Many successful triathlon winners and bodybuilders are vegetarians. I am 6 foot 3 inches tall, weigh over 14 stone and can hold a pencil unaided. I don't eat meat.

## ROMAN HOLIDAY

My husband and I recently went to Rome for our 5th wedding anniversary. On our first evening there, while I was looking out of the hotel window admiring the view, my husband came up behind me and stood beside me caressing my bottom. I was wearing a very thin silky dress and we both got quite turned on. Before I knew what was happening he had pulled down my knickers, pushed up my dress, moved behind me and unzipped his trousers. We then made love with me leaning on the window sill and him standing behind me. I found it very exciting, particularly because I was in full view of the people passing by just below our window. Although no one could see anything they shouldn't have seen, I suspect that quite a few people knew exactly what we were doing. We repeated this experience twice and on one occasion, at night, I stood in the window naked while my husband made love to me from behind. I found making love in public very exciting. Since coming home we have made love in the park, on a train, in a multi storey car park and in one of the old fashioned telephone kiosks (I don't think it would be possible in one of the new ones). Could we get into trouble doing this?

Only if someone who sees you complains and you get caught. And then, even if the court shows you mercy, the resulting publicity could be embarrassing. You could, I suppose, always claim that you were both suffering from hypothermia—and were trying to warm one another up.

You weren't in Rome on February 17th were you? Do you have a little butterfly tattoo on your left breast? If that was you I've got some wonderful photos you might like.

........................................................

## SUCKLING HUBBY

I have had two children and breast fed them without any problems. Recently, for no apparent reason, my breasts have started to produce lots of milk again. I am not pregnant and my doctor says that there is nothing at all wrong with me. There is so much milk that I have to get my husband to relieve me. He doesn't mind at all—in fact he says he enjoys it. I have used a pump to empty them but I do not get the same sense of relief as I get when my husband suckles me. Is this anything to worry about?

It is nothing to worry about at all—though if your husband keeps sucking, the milk will probably keep coming. It is common for women to enjoy being suckled by their lovers. Some women have a baby on one breast and a partner on the other. Many women report that milk leaks out of their breasts if they become sexually aroused. One told me that milk always spurted out of her breasts whenever she had an orgasm. If there is too much milk for your husband to cope with you could become a donor to your local milk bank (the modern form of 'wet nursing'—your local maternity hospital may have one). The only possible problem I can think of is that you might have to buy your husband a dummy if the milk ever does stop coming. This could cause him some slight embarrassment on the commuter train to work.

...........................................................................

## NOISE IN THE BEDROOM

I am 33 years old and have been married for ten years. For some time I have not been very interested in sex. When my husband approaches me I make excuses to avoid it.
I recently came home early from work. I went into the house quietly as my husband was in bed after his night shift. As I went upstairs I heard a noise in the bedroom. I peered in through the crack between the door and the door frame and saw my husband lying naked on the bed wearing a pair of my stockings and playing with himself. I quickly and quietly went back downstairs and opened and closed the door as though I had just come in. My husband got up and acted as if nothing had happened.
That night, when he had gone to work I lay in bed thinking of what had I had seen. I have to admit that I was very excited by it. The thought of him in my underwear excited me a lot. I masturbated to a climax very quickly.
Do you think I should tell him what I saw as I think it would help our sex life. The thought of making love to him dressed up is a real turn on for me.

I don't think you should tell him that you saw him. He might be embarrassed. But why don't you bring the subject up as though it was your idea? You could, for example, say that you'd seen a letter or an article about men who wear women's clothing and you had wondered whether he had ever fancied the idea. You can hint that you had found the thought a turn on. The moment has to be right, of course. Lying in bed together is a good moment. Sitting round the table entertaining the in-laws is not a good moment.

## BY APPOINTMENT

Getting an appointment to see my doctor is like getting an audience with the Pope. This morning my little boy woke up with a terrible sore throat and because he suffers a lot with throat and ear problems I rang the surgery. The receptionist offered me an appointment in a fortnight's time! What do you suggest I do? Please don't suggest that I change doctors. There is only one convenient doctors' surgery.

Patients who are ill (as opposed to needing repeat prescriptions, check ups, insurance examinations and so on) should always be able to get an appointment within 24 hours at most. If you explained to the receptionist that the problem was urgent, and you didn't specify a particular doctor or a particular time of day, you have every right to feel very aggrieved. Next time this happens tell the receptionist that if the doctor can't see your son at the surgery then you want a home visit. The chances are that the receptionist will, miraculously, find a vacant appointment.

## WET, WET, WET

A few days ago I was watching TV with my fiancé and his parents when I laughed so much that I wet myself. I am 24 and I did feel very ashamed but I honestly could not help myself. It was very embarrassing. I wet the sofa and had to travel home with wet underwear and wet skirt. To make things even worse my fiance has broken off our engagement. He told me that his mother says I am incontinent and will smell all the time. When I visited my doctor he said he could find nothing wrong and just laughed at me. He said I'd have to wear nappies or waterproof panties and I cried all the way home. Please tell me, is what happened to me odd for a girl of my age? This has happened once or twice to me before—usually when I have been laughing or coughing.

I felt sad and happy for you when I read your letter. Sad because you suffer from occasional incontinence and because your fiancé's mother has a mouth the size of the Channel Tunnel entrance, your former boyfriend is as loveable as silage and your doctor seems to be about as full of understanding and compassion as a lawyer with toothache. But happy for you because you seem to have had a narrow escape from a pretty awful marriage.

Incontinence is common—I get a lot of letters about it. One in five women wet themselves if they laugh, cry or cough too much. Next time you see five women in a queue remember that the chances are that one of the five suffers from incontinence.

The good news is that if there really is nothing wrong with you (and if you are in any doubt then it might be sensible to get your doctor to refer you to a more competent physician) then there is an exercise you can do which will help you strengthen the muscles around your bladder and reduce your chances of suffering from incontinence in the future (it will also mean that you'll have a sizzling sex life when you find a new and more understanding boyfriend).

## SIXTY

I am sixty years old. I masturbate with the aid of a vibrator at least four times a week when I have a sudden urge for sex. Is this harmful to me or is there any cure I could have.

It is not harmful. There is no need for a cure. Just make sure you keep in a supply of spare batteries.

## Socks on

My boyfriend always keeps his socks on when we make
love. I find this a real turn-off. How can I stop him.

Try wearing a woolly vest, long johns and a woolly bobble
hat next time he's feeling amorous.

## Flat nose

I am black and I need to wear spectacles. My nose is very
flat and they won't stay on. Do you have any suggestions?

Keep your spectacles in place with an elasticated band
that goes round the back of your head. If your optician
doesn't sell them you should be able to get one from a sports
shop.

## Dinner with the boss

Two months ago I gave up eating meat. Last Saturday my
husband and I were invited to dinner with his boss. I had
sent a note to say that I am vegetarian but when the main
course was served it turned out to be steak. There was no
vegetarian alternative. I was horrified and after hesitating
for a moment or two eventually plucked up courage to
remind my boss's wife that I didn't eat meat and ask if she
would mind if I just ate the vegetables. I didn't want her to
make anything special for me. Much to my embarrassment
she got quite nasty about it and asked me if I had just
given up meat because I thought it was fashionable. She
also told us how much the steak had cost. Her husband
made some comment about starving millions in Africa. My
husband then actually apologised on my behalf! He said
I sometimes did allow my emotions to rule my head. I felt
about half an inch tall. In the end I felt so miserable and
embarrassed that I ate the meat even though every
mouthful made me feel sick. My husband later told me that

after the meal his boss had taken him to one side and warned him that if I was going to behave like that at future functions it would be better if he left me at home. When we got home we had a big row about it. My husband said that I could have damaged his chances of promotion. Do you think I was being reasonable? What should I have done?

In your position at that dinner party, reasonable behaviour would have been to throw your food at the wall and walk out. I think you would have been quite justified in tearing the heads off your host and hostess and stuffing the entire meal down their throats. Your letter made me furious on your behalf. Who the hell did these people think they were to force you swallow your principles along with their damned steak?

And what sort of wimpy, white livered, limp lipped, chinless apology for a man are you married to? Who does he work for? The Gestapo? I think you should leave your husband instantly. Your husband's boss and his wife you can ignore. They need play no further part in your life. But no one should have to stay married to a partner who behaves as your husband did.

## PILL AFTER SEX

First, is it true that it is possible to take a pill after sex to stop a pregnancy happening? Second, does a doctor have a responsibility to provide any such pill? I had sex with my boyfriend three months ago and the condom we were using split. My boyfriend said he thought there was a pill available I could take so I immediately rang my doctor's surgery. The doctor who was on call refused to help me and said that if I had sex then I should be prepared to have a baby. I now think I could be pregnant. I have found out that the doctor who refused to help me is a Catholic and opposes contraception of any kind.

Yes, it is possible to take a pill to stop a pregnancy developing—though the pills need to be taken no later than 72 hours after sex. The most common side effects are nausea and vomiting. A patient who misses the 72-hour deadline for some reason can have an intra uterine contraceptive device (an IUCD) inserted up to 5 days after sex and that will usually stop a pregnancy developing.

(Why would anyone miss the 72-hour deadline? I have this awful vision of a woman turning up in a doctor's surgery and saying: 'I've just discovered I had sex four days ago. Is it too late to give me something to stop me getting pregnant?')

Some doctors are unwilling to provide any sort of contraceptive advice for personal (usually religious) reasons. Your doctor's refusal to help could well have been inspired by his or her own religious beliefs.

My view is that if a doctor won't help a patient because of his or her personal beliefs then he or she *must* find an alternative practitioner who will provide help.

Meanwhile, you have to make a vital decision.

Do you want to have your pregnancy terminated?

If you do then you should contact a sympathetic doctor immediately.

If, however, you want to become a mother then you should see your doctor about attending ante-natal classes.

One final thought: much as I hate lawyers, I suppose you could try sueing the doctor who wouldn't help you, either for the cost of bringing up the child you presumably didn't want and needn't have had if you had been provided with post-coital contraception, or for the trauma of having to have an abortion.

The legal arguments over that one could probably keep the courts busy for a decade at least.

## GOOD CHRISTIAN PARENTS

We are Good Christian Parents and we strongly object to some of the sexual content of your column. Some of the letters you print are from depraved people who deserve to rot in hell.

I have received tens of thousands of letters since I started writing this column. Less than half a dozen have been letters of complaint. Three of those have been anonymous letters from people who describe themselves as Good Christian Parents (always with the capital letters). I am reminded of a comment the American musician Frank Zappa made. He pointed out that the Kama Sutra hasn't killed anywhere near as many people as The Bible has. Sexual problems are as much a part of life as indigestion, arthritis and piles. People who describe themselves as Good Christian Parents are now banned from reading this column. Go away. I don't want you reading my pages.

## STAG NIGHT

I am getting married in two months time. The only thing that worries me is that my best man has told me that he is organising a stag night for me. All my mates have stag nights and they invariably get completely wild. At the last stag night party I went to there were a couple of cheap hookers present. After the groom had done it with them most of the rest of blokes did it too—in full view of everyone else. Even though I was turned on by it all, I didn't do anything because I am ashamed of my penis which is very small and slightly bent when erect.

Afterwards we all got absolutely smashed, stole some cars and drove around the streets banging on the car horns and sticking our bums out of the windows. It was a great night. What worries me is that on my stag night I won't be able to avoid exposing my private parts. Although they are my mates I know they will laugh at me.

Can you recommend something I can do to enlarge the size of my penis?

I know of no reliable method by which you can permanently increase the size of your bent and shrunken organ.

I'm relieved that you are worried about something important and not allowing yourself to lose sleep over something trivial like the risk of contracting a disease you can pass on to your bride on your wedding night.

I wonder why you feel you have to attend a party that fills you with such dread.

Have you thought about saying something subtle like: 'No, thanks. I don't want a stag party.'

No, I don't suppose you have.

And even if you had, saying 'No' would probably require far too complex an inter-reaction between brain and mouth.

It is when I get letters from people like you—exhibiting all the wit, insight and moral courage of a diseased and discarded nail clipping—that I realise why we have the Government we have. It's frightening to think that people like you and your mates have the vote.

What a selfish little piece of sewage you are.

I hope your penis develops a temporary wasting disease and shrivels up to the size of a pin on your big night out with the lads.

Does that help?

..........................................................................................

## PERIODS OF PAIN

I am a 17-year-old girl. I am taking my school examinations very soon. The trouble is that for most of the exams I will be on my period. The result will be disastrous, I know. During my periods I can't concentrate and I suffer quite a lot of pain. My whole future depends on these exams because if I do not get the right results I will not be able to go to college. I have heard that the contraceptive pill can be used to control period pains but I am afraid that if I start taking this my mother will get the wrong idea.

I think the contraceptive pill is the best solution. Go and see your family doctor and tell him exactly what you've told me. He can ask the pharmacist to dispense the pills in an ordinary brown bottle rather than in the usual contraceptive pack. Then explain to your mother that the pills are just to control your period pain. No lies and no misconceptions.

## MOODY

My boyfriend is always a bit moody after we have made love. Is this normal?

Yes. Normalish. It isn't anything to worry about—as long as you get on well together the rest of the time. It's all to do with male hormones and blood flow. It's also normal for men to feel tired and fall asleep after making love. It is, however, considered polite for a man who has been making love in the missionary position to clamber off his partner before starting to snore.

## UNAVOIDABLY AROUSED

I am a 52-year-old married lecturer. Six weeks ago one of my students came to see me for a tutorial. She was wearing very tight jeans and a white blouse. The top four buttons of the blouse were undone and it was quite clear that she was not wearing anything underneath it. I was unavoidably aroused and when, during the tutorial, she made it very clear that she was willing to make love to me I'm afraid that I was foolish enough to succumbed to temptation. She has now told me that unless I give her good marks and ensure that she obtains a good degree she will make a formal complaint about me to the university. If she does this there is a good chance that I will lose my job. I have never done anything like this before and I have no idea what to do now. I would very much appreciate any advice you can give me. I cannot deny that we made love because I have a physical abnormality in a very private place and I know she is aware of this. I have no intention of giving in to her blackmail whatever the consequences. I have thought about complaining to the police but decided against it. If I give her the mark she deserves she will fail though she is a bright student and if she worked hard she could almost certainly pass.

She wants to get her degree and you want to avoid trouble. Why not offer to coach her so that she gets the marks she needs? (But keep your eyes off her cleavage and have your trousers sewn up). In the meantime cover the options by joining a nudist club or taking a lot of showers at a sports club. If you make sure that plenty of strangers have a chance to view your physical abnormality her potentially deadly piece of evidence will shrink in importance.

## AFFAIR AT WORK

Two months ago I found out that my wife had been having an affair with a man she works with. I was devastated. The affair had been going on for two years but I had never suspected anything. When my wife found out she broke down, cried a lot and said she wouldn't see him again. As far as I know she hasn't. She even left her job so that she wouldn't have to see him. But she is now making my life miserable. We don't have much money and she says that is my fault because she gave up her job to please me (I didn't ask her to). She complains about everything I do and seems to delight in criticising and belittling me. In my heart I know that the problem is that she still loves this other fellow—and only came back to me through a sense of duty. I don't know what to do though I know I can't go on like this even though I do still love her. I think I would rather we parted than carried on the way we are. What do you suggest?

You have to think carefully about what you want. Would you rather lose your wife than live with her as things are?

If you decide that you really can't go on with things the way they are then you must talk things through with your wife.

Ask her if she loves you or the other man. Ask her to be honest with you. And tell her how you feel.

There will be a lot of tears and a lot of pain. And you may end up losing your wife.

But maybe you've lost her already.

I suspect you may be right. Your wife may still be in love with the other man. And she may be punishing you for what has happened. She almost certainly feels miserable and guilty. Consciously or not she wants you to suffer. That is no basis for any sort of relationship.

But there is a chance that talking will help.

Maybe she loves you too. Maybe the other man doesn't love her. Maybe she needs time to sort her own mind out.

One possible solution might be for the two of you to live apart for a while.

························································

## JUST ONE SNAG

Six months ago I met a girl and fell in love with her. I now live with her and we are both very happy. There is just one snag: I work as a plumber and my girl friend's father has an important job in advertising and does not hide the fact that he doesn't approve of me. Whenever I meet him he manages to make me feel about three inches tall by making snide and clever comments about ball-cocks, U bends and blocked lavatories. I served quite a long apprenticeship but in his company I always feel ashamed of what I do. Do you think our relationship can last? How should I deal with my girl-friend's father?

It's strange to think of someone who works in advertising having the nerve to look down on someone else. It's difficult to think of a job that merits less respect than that of advertising executive. Being a lawyer, perhaps.

First, you need to build up your self respect. You have a skilled and worthwhile job. Take pride in what you do. Try to rise above cheap taunts. Second, don't let your girlfriend's father con you into believing that what he does is important or worthwhile. Next time you see him ask him how he has spent his day. Get him to tell you about his clever campaigns for toilet paper, sanitary towels or dog food. Ask him to tell you exactly what he does. Third, talk to your girlfriend. Tell her how you feel. If she loves you then she will be sympathetic and her father's gross behaviour will do your relationship no harm.

One solution may be to see your girlfriend's father only when there are lots of other people around.

........................................................................

## POSSIBLE OR NOT?

Is it possible for a woman to get pregnant after having oral sex? My friend says it is possible. I say it isn't. Who's right?

Your friend. If the woman performs oral sex on the man and he ejaculates into her mouth and she kisses him and some of the sperm get into his mouth and he then performs oral sex on her—then she could get pregnant. It is also possible that I will sail single handed across the Atlantic in a bathtub. Both possibilities are remote.

........................................................................

## NO KNICKERS

I never wear knickers because I find that if I do I get thrush. I recently got married and my husband, who used to like the idea of me not wearing knickers before we got married, now objects. Do you think I am being unreasonable in continuing to go out without knickers on?

You are only being unreasonable if you wear flimsy skirts in windy weather, ride a bicycle in a short skirt or walk around on your hands.

Try telling your husband that if you wear knickers you'll get thrush and that will mean no sex.

......................................................

## TOO OLD?

Is there any age at which sex becomes a dirty word between husband and wife?

One hundred and seventy-nine.

......................................................

## LOVING SON

I am 37 and have a 22-year-old son. My husband left me when my baby was born. I am financially comfortable and my son has a good job. He is tall, fit and strong and plays football and cricket. My problem is that he has always slept with me and since he was 16 we have had a sexual relationship. There are times when I have an almost overwhelming urge to have his baby. He is quite willing and keen to have a baby with me. Would you please tell me what my prospects are of having a normal child. We are both in good health. I know that if I wait much longer I will be too old.

I don't think you should have a baby by your son. Every one of us carries at least one gene for a harmful disorder—and probably at least two for conditions that would result in a dead baby. Since you and your son may carry the same genes the risk of you giving birth to a dead or seriously deformed or mentally retarded baby is around 1 in 2. Those are terrible odds.

## MILK PRODUCTION

I have two children aged 21 and 19. I produced a lot of milk after they were born. My marriage broke up some time ago and I have a new partner. My problem is that I produce a lot of milk when we make love. Is this anything that I should worry about? Do you think it could be caused by the fact that my partner pays a lot of attention to my breasts? If it is not anything to worry about then I do not want to do anything about it because the fact that I produce milk is quite a turn on for my partner, and consequently for myself.

There probably isn't any reason at all to worry but I think you should see your doctor and let him check your nipples—and the discharge you are producing.

## SERIOUS RELATIONSHIP WANTED

I would love to have serious relationships with girls but I just can't find a way to talk to one, let alone ask one out. All I do is masturbate over pictures of nude women and fantasise about what might be. I sometimes wish I was a woman because then I would not have to make the first move. I would be very romantic and loving if I had a girl friend but I don't know how to start. I am 18 and embarrassed about the fact that I still have not even kissed a girl. I go to discos but find it impossible to pluck up the courage to talk to girls.

Don't kid yourself that girls don't have any anxieties. Millions of girls worry just as much as you do about finding a partner. Take the pressure off yourself. Instead of going to discos join clubs, societies and evening classes where you can meet and talk to people of both sexes.

## ORAL SEX WORRIES

Is it possible to contract a sexually transmitted disease by having oral sex? If it is then surely oral sex is a dangerous practice that should be avoided.

If one or both partners has an infection then it can be transmitted via oral sex. But that doesn't make oral sex a dangerous practice to avoid. Sexually transmitted diseases can, of course, be passed on through ordinary sex too. Any form of sex is only healthy when both partners are healthy.

........................................................................................

## WALKED OUT

My girl friend, who is carrying my baby, has walked out on me and gone back to her husband who lives nearby. I can't understand this because I have always been very kind to her and her husband beats her. I think she has probably gone back because her family have made her feel bad about being with me. Her three sons by her husband are all in their late teens and they have threatened me and called her names for leaving home. Two of her sons have hit her. I am very confused and unhappy and don't know what to do.

Talk to your girlfriend. If you can't talk to her then write to her. Ask her to think about what she wants—and about what she thinks will be best for the baby. She is undoubtedly very confused, too. If you put pressure on her then that could make things worse for her. Tell her how you feel about her and the baby and tell her that you will wait for her to make up her mind about who she wants to be with. Maybe you could suggest that if she wants to then the two of you will move away and start again somewhere else.

........................................................................................

## NO KIDS PLEASE

Neither I nor my boyfriend want children. To be honest we don't like children very much. Recently, when my mother asked me when I was going to have a baby I told her this. Since then she has never stopped nagging me about it.

She says that I am being very selfish in denying her grand-children and says that I have a duty and a responsibility to have at least one or two babies. She says that all women have a maternal instinct and that if I get pregnant I will grow to love my baby. Is this true and if so how do I persuade my boyfriend that we should start a family? Alternatively, how can I persuade my mother to believe me when I say that I really don't want to have a baby.

Don't let your mother push you around. And don't believe that old nonsense about all women having a deep, inbuilt maternal instinct. It is rubbish. Millions of women love children. But lots of women dislike children. And lots of women hate children. Moreover—sit down, brace yourself and prepare for a shock—lots of women secretly hate, despise and resent their own children. It's probably one of the biggest and best kept secrets of all time. It's something that is never discussed in public. But it is true, even though very few women would dare admit it in public—or, I suspect, even admit it privately to themselves.

Having a baby is a decision which you and your boyfriend should make together. Your mother should have no say in the matter. Nor should your boyfriend's mother. Nor should the milkman, the woman in the corner shop or your cousin's uncle's aunt.

If you really don't want children, if you really dislike children, then for heaven's sake stick to your guns.

If you had a really strong maternal instinct then you would probably feel broody when you picked up a friend's baby. So try it. Both of you. Go round and spend an evening with friends who have a baby (or preferably two). If, at the end of the evening, you look into each other's eyes and honestly say: 'Oh, wouldn't it wonderful to have a baby of our own!' then by all means rush home and get to work.

But if the smell of baby milk, talcum powder and dirty nappies fills you with a deep sense of dread, and you find yourselves breathing a sigh of relief when you walk out of your friend's home, then think very strongly indeed before you plunge into pregnancy. Once you start it isn't easy to go back. Remember: like a dog, a baby is for life.

········································································

## I AM GAY

I am gay and have been living with another man for three years. Last weekend the two of us went to stay with my sister (who is divorced) so that I could attend a family wedding. On the Friday afternoon I went shopping for a present and when I got back to the house I found my boyfriend in bed with my sister. I didn't even know that my boyfriend was bisexual and he hadn't met my sister until that afternoon. My boyfriend wanted me to join them in bed but I refused, even though my sister seemed quite happy about it. I thought the idea was totally disgusting. The idea of touching any naked woman makes me want to shudder. My boyfriend now says that he wants the three of us to live together. My sister says she's happy to give up her home to come and live with us and I'm in a total turmoil. I don't want to lose my boyfriend so I've said 'yes' but I'm not sure that I can get used to the idea of sharing him with a woman—let alone my sister. I've told my boyfriend that my sister will have to have her own bedroom and he will have to just sleep with us in turn. I know you can't decide my life for me but I would appreciate any advice you can give me. The funny thing is that I've never really got on very well with my sister. Until she got divorced I had hardly seen her for years because her former husband (whom I had always strongly suspected of being a closet gay) said he didn't like gays.

I think you all need to spend some time thinking and talking this through. Unless it is too late I certainly don't think that your sister should give up her home just yet.

Maybe you could suggest a trial period of a month just to see what happens.

If both your sister and your boyfriend remain determined to set up this *ménage à trois*, and you don't want to leave your boyfriend, then you are, I suppose, going to have to make the best of a rather unusual situation. If that happens then you should at least insist on some fairly clearly defined rules about where who does what with or to whom and when. Your proposal that your sister should have her own room is, for example, an excellent and sensible starting point.

## FIT TO DROP

Since I joined an aerobics class I've been injured twice and off work three times with infections. I've noticed that the other people who exercise with me are also sick quite often. I thought exercise would should make us all healthier! Can you explain what has gone wrong?

Being fit and being healthy aren't necessarily the same thing at all. Regular, gentle exercise that you enjoy will make you fit. But too much exercise—particularly if it is too strenuous or unduly competitive—can make you ill. Lots of very fit athletes are really unhealthy. How many young, professional sportsmen and women can go through a whole season without injury or illness? You should never exercise when you are ill. You should never do any form of exercise you don't enjoy. And you should never do any exercise that is painful. Follow these simple rules and there is a good chance that your exercise programme will make you fit *and* healthy.

## THREE STRANGERS

Two weeks ago my husband brought home three strangers from the pub. All four of them were drunk. My husband insisted that I make them some sandwiches and get them some more drinks. I was in the kitchen in my dressing gown, with only a flimsy nightie underneath it, when suddenly my husband unfastened the cord at the front and exposed me. He then laughed, made a rude remark and invited one of the men to touch my breasts. I tried to stop them but my husband helped to hold me still while the three strangers all had sex with me. When the three men had finished my husband did it too. The next morning my husband told me that if I said anything he would beat me up. I know he means it because he has done it in the past. The next Saturday he did the same thing only this time there were four strangers. He says he is going to bring home different men every Saturday night because it turns him on to see strangers having sex with me. He is a big man and when he is drunk he is terrifying. I have one friend and when I told her she said I should tell the police. I don't know what to do. I have two small children and no money of my own.

I confess I don't know whether to suggest that you contact the police or not. Technically, you were undoubtedly raped on both occasions. But the police will want to know why you didn't report the rapes closer to the time. And your husband and the men who raped you will undoubtedly claim that you were willing. On balance, if you pushed me to make a specific recommendation, I would tell you not to bother going to the police. But I would—and do—suggest that you get in touch with your nearest refuge for battered wives. Your local social services department or citizens' advice bureau should be able to help you with an address or telephone number.

I think you have to leave your husband and to try to forget that you were ever married to him or had children by him. If you have relatives or friends in another town who will look after you then leave town. Some people would say that you have done nothing wrong and that you should stay and stick up for yourself. Unfortunately, there is a big gap between justice and the law. If you stay and fight you could fall through that gap. Running away might well be your best bet. Get your doctor to check that you haven't been infected or made pregnant. Take care and good luck.

## MORE VULNERABLE

Do you think the human immune system is becoming weaker? Everyone I know seems to suffer from far more infections than we used to when I was little.

Yes, I think we are more vulnerable to infections these days. There are several reasons. We don't eat as well our grandparents did (we eat a lot of nicely packaged junk TV food that has all the vitamins taken out of it). We live and work in centrally heated, air conditioned buildings which circulate bugs and damage our ability to cope with cold weather. We're under far more stress and pressure. And, to top it all, doctors have overprescribed antibiotics so wildly that the bugs have become resistant to them. This means that when we do fall ill we take longer to get better. I suggest that to increase your resistance to infection you eat plenty of fresh fruit and green vegetables, turn down your central heating and try to keep out of air conditioned buildings.

## SLEEPING VIRGIN

My boyfriend and I have slept together and I have let him put his penis into my vagina a little way but I have never let him put it all the way in. This means that I am still a virgin doesn't it?

Yes, you're a virgin, the Government is firmly in charge of the economy, my Dad has a full head of hair and the world is free of crime and greed. Who are you trying to kid? You can't be a bit of a virgin any more than you can be a bit pregnant or a bit dead. Try to remember that even though you may think of yourself as still a virgin you can get pregnant and catch infectious diseases by doing what you're doing.

## Hanging loose

Why do my boyfriend's testicles sometimes hang loose and sometimes tuck tightly into his body?

They hang loose when they're hot and want to cool down. When they're cold they climb up to get warm. Testicles also tuck in tight when their owner is frightened, nervous or about to orgasm.

## Different sizes

Is it true that most women have one breast slightly bigger than the other? My left breast is bigger than my right one. Could the fact that I am left handed and play a lot of tennis explain this?

It is rare to find a woman whose breasts are both exactly the same size—so it could be that your left breast is naturally larger. But if you've built up more muscles on the left side of your chest that would make your left breast appear larger. If it worries you get a good coach to give you some exercises to build up the muscles on the other side of your chest.

## Extra money

I am a student and I have been working in a bar to make some money. On Saturdays I get triple pay to work topless. Last Saturday a customer offered me £30 to go back to his hotel with him after I had finished work. I didn't go but after talking to one or two of the other girls I found that offers like this are not uncommon. One girl says she has a customer nearly every Saturday night and gets paid £100 for a couple of hours 'work'. She says it isn't prostitution and we can't get into trouble with the police if we only do it once a week. Is this true?

Someone who accepts money to go to bed with someone else is a prostitute. It doesn't matter whether you do it once a week, once a lifetime or once a minute. And it doesn't matter how much you charge, either. A woman who accepts £5 is a prostitute just as much as one who charges £1,000 a night. She's just not as good at it. But surely the legality (or illegality) of what you're clearly thinking of doing is only part of all this. Selling sex is easy money but what about the risk of disease? And if you do get caught how will that affect your career prospects? Remember, too, that if you start working as a prostitute you will expose yourself to all sorts of horrible dangers—both from pimps and nutty customers. Who knows, you could end up going to bed with a politician! Working topless is one thing but selling your body is a big step down the line. You must do whatever you think is right. But do think through the consequences before you start.

........................................................................

## MORE ROMANCE, PLEASE

My boyfriend treats me like an equal. He insists on us sharing the cost whenever go out together but to be honest I'd prefer it if he paid (even if I gave him the money afterwards). He has never bought me chocolates or flowers. I would like him to be more romantic and to me that includes being assertive and maybe even domineering but I am not sure how to tell him this without hurting his feelings.

Have you tried telling him what you want? Have you tried hinting? Have you tried manipulation? You're a woman, for God's sake. Surely you don't need me to tell you how to manipulate a man! Next time you're going out together give him enough money to cover your half of the expenses. Then just let him take over and make all the decisions. Afterwards, reward him for his effort in the way you know he likes best. Who knows, before you know it he may be opening doors for you on a regular basis. But watch out—he may get to like being in charge.

## DONE WELL

I am sixty seven years old and have done well in life, thanks to nobody but myself. My wife is three years younger than I and we have been married for 45 years. Both our children are grown up and self sufficient. I have quite a decent amount in the bank and I paid off the mortgage a long time ago. However, my wife has become very lazy. I take her out on her birthday and take her on holiday every year but I get little satisfaction from doing this because my wife takes this kind of thing for granted. I give her housekeeping money when she asks for it as long as she gives me the receipts for what she has bought. She is not as attractive as she used to be and since she does not seem interested in sex I get my satisfaction elsewhere. She says I am being unreasonable in expecting her to go out and get a job but I have done my job properly and I believe it is her responsibility to pull her weight. After all I have had to work very hard to make myself financially secure. Why should she get an easy ride?

What a unique approach you have to marriage. I checked the postmark on your letter half expecting to find that it had been posted from Mars or had been stuck in the postal system for a century or so. You weren't a victim of some bizarre, nineteenth-century scientific experiment, were you?

All over the country thousands of grateful men will now be reading your letter out loud to their wives, ever thankful to you for making them seem like good fellows.

My advice to you is to buy yourself a crash hat and a bullet and knife proof flak jacket and to wear them both night and day just in case your wife finally cracks.

## MY SON'S FRIEND

I am a 37-year-old divorced woman with an 18-year-old son who has just started college. Last weekend my son came home for the first time and brought a friend with him. On Sunday morning I had to go into the room in which my son's friend was staying to get something out of a cupboard. I knocked on the door, went in, got what I wanted and then looked round to see that my son's friend had pushed back the bed clothes and was lying there quite naked with a very noticeable erection. I blushed when I saw it because it has been several years since I saw a man in that state. He then asked me to fondle him. I didn't really want to but I'm afraid I couldn't help myself. I put down the things I'd collected and sat on the edge of the bed. I then played with my son's friend until he came while he fondled my breasts through my jumper. When I left the bedroom I was so aroused that I had to lock myself in my room for a while. I'm sure you can imagine why. Neither of us said anything about it afterwards but when he left my son's friend thanked me and said he hoped I'd let him come to stay again. My son has rung twice since but he hasn't mentioned his friend and I haven't mentioned him either, of course. However, I find myself thinking about him all the time and if he does come back to stay I just know I will find an excuse to go into his room again. I really don't know what to do. Part of me wants to try and get in touch with the boy to see if we can develop some sort of relationship, after all the age difference isn't all that great. I have got several friends who have been out with men much younger than they are. My sister lives with a man who is 12 years younger than her. Part of me says this is crazy and I should just forget all about him. What do you think I should do?

I hate to be brutal but I'm afraid I think you should try to forget about him. It doesn't sound to me as if your son's friend really wanted a proper relationship so much as a quick thrill. And think about your son. If you start an affair with his chum what is that going to do to your relationship with him? Age need not be a barrier to love but, sadly, I don't really think this sounds like a romance made in heaven.

· · · · · · · · · · · · · · · · · · · · · · · · · · · · · · · · · · · · · · · · · · · · · · · · · · · · ·

## GOLF BALLS

I work as a golf professional and women at the club where I work often make it pretty clear that they fancy me. So far this year I have been to bed with at least a dozen different women. However, I have now found myself in a difficult position. I was giving a lesson to a woman the other day when she bluntly told me that she wanted me to go back to her home with her. I didn't fancy her at all (she is fat, has a noticeable moustache and smells terrible) so I said 'no' but she shocked me by saying that if I didn't do what she wants she would tell my wife about the other women I've seen. Apparently one or two of the woman have been talking in the women's changing rooms. When I pointed out that this was blackmail she laughed and agreed with me. I think she means business. Can you think of a way I can get out of this?

You have three choices.

1. You can grit your teeth, close your eyes and go to bed with the smelly woman with the moustache (and every other sex starved member who wants to take advantage of your body). If you take this option then within six months you will almost certainly be suffering from permanent impotence. Locker room chatter will quickly destroy your reputation as a stud.

2. You can tell the smelly woman with the moustache to get stuffed with something or someone else and then close your eyes and wait for the sound and feel of bone splintering as your wife lets go with the rolling pin. The physical pain will be as nothing compared to the pain you have to endure when the lawyers start scrubbing your balls clean.

3. You can tell the smelly woman with the moustache to get stuffed and then rush home, confess all to your wife and beg her forgiveness for your twelve accidental indiscretions. You will then spend the next three years putting up shelves, cleaning out the garage and generally

becoming a nauseatingly grateful slave to your wife's every whim.

What a pity that you should get bunkered after scoring so well. I'm sure that other readers will share my shallow and unconvincing concern at your predicament. We will all be fascinated to know which of these agonies you choose to endure.

## SEVEN WOMEN

Two months ago I had my first ever lesbian relationship. Since then I have been to bed with seven women. Is it possible for a lesbian to catch any sexually transmitted diseases? I have been told that lesbianism is perfectly safe and that lesbians never catch diseases from one another— apart from things like colds, of course. Is this true?

No human activity is without risk. A man I know once knelt down to pray in church and impaled his knee upon a protruding nail. Your safety will depend upon how healthy your partners are and precisely what you do to one another, with what and in what order.

## REMEMBERING DREAMS

I'd love to be able to remember my dreams but I never can. Can you please tell me if there is any way in which I can make sure that I remember at least some of them?

Vary the time when you wake up—but go to bed at the same time. This way you'll greatly increase your chances of waking up during or just after a dream.

## FIDDLY, NOT SEXY

Why do men like women to wear stockings and suspenders? They are very fiddly and I don't think they are at all sexy.

I have no idea why men find stockings and suspenders sexy. They just do. I have a strong suspicion that the time when women stopped wearing stockings and suspenders and started to wear tights marked the end of modern civilisation. Practical women welcomed tights because they found them more comfortable than stockings (though they were soon also to find them less healthy). Feminists welcomed the banishing of stockings because they regarded them as sexist garb which trivialised women. I've no doubt both groups were right. But none of this alters the fact that if men think a woman is wearing stockings they think of her differently.

## SIZE MATTERS

Six of us (all women) were talking about penises in our break at work. We agreed that size (length and width), shape and colour are all very important. We all agreed that we are much more likely to have satisfying sex with a man who has got a big one. It's about time that old myth about it 'not being what you've got but what you do with it' was put to rest. What you do with it doesn't matter a damn if it isn't big enough in the first place. Why don't you have the guts to tell the truth? Are you worried that millions of your male readers will all be thrown into a state of total despair?

Yes. Since female readers have now had their say, what do men think: does the size of a woman's vagina influence a man's ability to enjoy sex?

Incidentally, those men who thought that women only ever discussed the best way to get their laundry looking really white now know the truth.

## COVETED ASS

Women always say they are jealous because I am so slim but I would rather be a bit fatter—in particular I'd like to have a bit more curve below the waist. My friend (who is four inches bigger than me around the hips) and I went to Italy recently and whereas she got chatted up all the time—and got her bottom pinched nearly every day—the only men I met were the friends of the men who pinched her bottom! How can I improve my shape?

You should remember the Tenth Commandment: Thou shalt not covet thy neighbour's ass. I bet your friend envies you your slim behind. The curve is always sweeter on the other woman's bottom. Female curves, whether above or below the waist, are made up largely of fat. If you want more curves you'll have to eat more—and get plumper. The snag is that God, not you, decides where the fat gets deposited.

························································

## DIRTY POST

My boyfriend is working away from home. He has asked me to post him personal items from my dirty laundry. In particular he wants me to send him my knickers and bras. I don't particularly mind sending him these things but I can't imagine what he wants them for. My first thought was that he might be a secret transvestite but he is much bigger than I am and I don't think he would fit into any of my underwear.

I don't think your boyfriend wants to wear your dirty underwear. (If he was a transvestite he wouldn't have stipulated that it be dirty). I have tried (in vain) to think of ways to be tasteful about this. Close your eyes everyone else. I think your boyfriend wants your underwear to help provide him with a little physical stimulation and sensory enhancement during solitary, manual sexual adventures. Are you with me? No? Oh dear. Can't you please find someone else to explain it to you? The rest of you can open your eyes again now, by the way.

## SIZE DIFFERENCE

I am only five foot tall and my husband is well over six foot tall and weighs nearly twice as much as me. We want to start a family but I am worried about the size difference between us. Will I be able to give birth to his child?

Your baby may grow up to be the same size as your husband but he or she is unlikely to start out that way. There is not necessarily any real correlation between the size of a baby and the size of the parents. The most important factor is the size of your pelvis. If you have nice, broad, womanly hips then giving birth will be easier.

## DEEP SEX

My boy friend wants me to try a new sexual position which he says will enable us to have really deep sex. He says that if I lie on my back and put my legs over his shoulders he will be able to push his penis a really long way into me. He says that deep penetration will be more satisfying for me because my cervix will be stimulated. He does not have a particularly large penis (in fact he is considerably smaller in that department than any of the other men I have been to bed with) but even so I'm a little worried that it might be painful. What do you think?

The position you describe is good for deep penetration. The only way to find out whether you like it or not is to try it. But be prepared to say 'no' if it hurts (and make sure your boyfriend knows what 'no' means). I wonder if he confusing your cervix with your clitoris? The former is the neck of your womb. The latter, the main stimulus for sexual excitement in women, is the small, pea sized gland above your vaginal entrance.

## 14 TIMES

Is it true that men think of sex at least 14 times every 5 minutes.

If it was it would explain why trains never run on time, why there are long queues at most high street banks and why the nation's economy is in such a mess. But I don't think it's true.

I doubt if the real figure is much above 11 or 12 times every 5 minutes.

## ONE IN FIVE

Why don't women have orgasms as easily as men? My boyfriend has an orgasm nearly every time we have sex. I'm lucky if I have an orgasm once in every five times. Why is this?

Because sex was originally designed as a procreative activity. If a woman is going to become pregnant it is essential that the man ejaculates—has an orgasm. But it doesn't matter a toss whether the woman has an orgasm or not. The mechanism for having an orgasm is there (basically it's the same as the orgasmic mechanism in the male) but, in the same way that the clitoris is rather rudimentary compared to the penis so the orgasmic equipment doesn't work quite as well in women. Please send any complaints about this direct to the manufacturer. I believe his offices are open on Sundays.

## A WASTED LIFE

My husband has never been anything but kind and considerate and loving but I feel that I have wasted my life. When I was a girl (I am in my 40s now) we were brought up to think of sex before marriage as wrong. So I was a virgin on my wedding night. Now I feel jealous when I see young couples walking along the street and I just know that even though they aren't married they are probably sleeping together. I am very lucky to have such a caring and gentle husband but I have started to wonder what would have happened if I had 'played around' a bit more before I'd got married. The truth is that our sex life has never been very good and I doubt if I would married the man I have spent my life with so far if I had had more partners when I was young.

You're going through the 'oh my god I'm over 40 and I wonder if I've wasted my life' syndrome. There's a constant epidemic of it in neat homes all over the country. The regrets take many different forms. Men usually wonder whether they'd have been happier if they hadn't got married, settled down and taken on responsibilities but had instead tried to make it as professional snooker stars, footballers, golfers or rock and roll stars. Your regrets about your missing sexual adventures are simply another sign of the passing years.

What would life have been like if you'd put it around a bit when you were 17? Heaven knows. I don't. Maybe you'd have met a racing driver and be living in Monaco by now. Maybe you'd have married a guy with a huge prick who gave you everlasting orgasms but turned out to be a huge prick himself. Maybe you would have caught syphilis, got pregnant at 18 and spent your life on the 45th floor of a council tower block. Maybe you'd have been forced into the white slave trade.

OK, you missed a few minutes of sexual pleasure when you were a teenager. So what? Even women who spend their teenage years leaping in and out of bed eventually spend more of their lives cleaning their teeth than do in having orgasmic sexual experiences. Sex is no more than a spice in the big meal of life. Your problem is not that you didn't get screwed enough when you were 17 but that your life today has no purpose. You're bored. You're thinking backwards because you haven't got any reason to think forwards.

The answer is to find yourself some passion. I don't mean an affair with the milkman. I mean real passion: a purpose for living. Find something you believe in and can fight for. You may be too old to start wearing a mini dress and no bra and picking up boys in discos but you aren't too old to find a purpose for your life. Get rid of the self pity, get off your complacent, spreading bottom and start changing the world. Only when you've found something you're prepared to die for will you really know what life is all about.

........................................................................

## Madly in love

I've fallen madly in love with my doctor. You may not think this is unusual but my doctor is a woman and I am a happily married woman with a lovely home and two beautiful children. I have never had feelings like this before and have never had any sort of relationship with a woman. Whenever I see her my heart beats so fast it almost jumps out of my chest. The way I feel I know I've never really been in love before. It is a wonderful feeling but I can't concentrate on anything else.

I suspect that you are enjoying a sexual fantasy. And if you are then you should be careful not to confuse fantasy with reality. Think it through. Imagine yourself telling your doctor that you love her. What do you think her reaction would be? And what would you do then? Can you see yourself running away with her? Do you see yourself setting up house together? Or is it all an unrealistic (but doubtless exciting) fantasy that has got a little out of hand? There's nothing wrong with fantasy as long as you don't let it get it mixed up with real life.

## PRIVATE PARTS

For a year now I have had no sexual feeling in my private parts. When my husband touches me down below it is no more exciting than if he was cutting my toe nails. Imagine trying to work yourself into a sexual frenzy while having your toe nails cut because that is what it is like for me. My doctor says there is nothing physically wrong with me and that it's all in my mind.

I think you need to take a trip into sexual-fantasy land. Next time your husband is puffing away 'cutting your toe nails' close your eyes and think of someone you fancy. Anyone. Dead, alive or somewhere in between. Anyone you'd really rather like to be naughty with. Let your mind wander. Be as devilish and shocking as you like. If this doesn't work then take up stamp collecting instead.

## STILL AT HOME

Our son who is 32 years old is still living at home. His only interests are boozing with the lads, gambling and sport—exactly the same as when he was in his teens. He doesn't seem much interested in women (though he isn't the other way either). We think he may have something wrong with him. How can we jolt him into facing up to reality and accepting his responsibilities like other men of his age?

Let me get this straight. Your son is 32 and still having his cooking and laundry done by his mum. He pays a nominal sum towards the housekeeping and spends most of his money on boozing and gambling and generally having a good time. And you think there's something wrong with him? You feel he should spend more of his time cutting the lawn, putting up shelves, pushing a shopping trolley around the supermarket and buying £90 trainers for kids who think more of the TV than they do of him?

Well, I hate to tell you this but I can find approximately

20 million men who will argue that your son is perfectly sane and that everyone else in the world is a couple of politicians short of a party. I suspect that he will only start taking life seriously when you kick him out and force him to find someone else to darn his socks and put his milk in his tea for him.

## SEXUALLY IMPOTENT

If a man has a heart attack could it make him sexually impotent for five years? Or do you think he is using it as an excuse?

There is no specific reason why a man who has a heart attack should become impotent. However, having a heart attack can be pretty frightening. And many heart attack victims deliberately avoid doing things which they fear may trigger off another attack. I suggest that you get your husband (it is your husband we're talking about, isn't it?) to see his doctor. If the doctor says that sex is OK then experiment with positions (him lying on his back and you gently lowering yourself down onto him for example) in which you do most of the work and he just lies there and enjoys it.

## 19 YEARS AFTER

My sister's husband has been having an affair for 19 years. My sister had known about it for 12 years. The family decided to put a stop to it. We wrote letters to her boss and we wrote to her husband at his work. We phoned her children and wrote to all her neighbours. But the two guilty parties both denied it. Then we wrote to his boss and neighbours. He thought she had done it and so he beat her up. The problem is that she has now started writing nasty letters about us. She has written to my sister's neighbours. Is there anything we can do to have her stopped?

What's all this about 'the family'? Do all the men wear dark suits and carry violin cases? Are all the women large bosomed and do they spend their days cooking spaghetti?

You started the war and now that the opposition have started firing back you don't like it. Has it ever occurred to you that a relationship (albeit an illicit one) that lasts for 19 years must have meant something? Have you asked your sister why she didn't do anything for 12 years? Did you worry about the damage you might do by contacting this woman's children?

I'm not going to take sides but it seems to me that if you really want to stop all this nonsense you could start with a bunch of flowers, an apology and a handshake. Assuming that you don't intend to start opening the violin cases I think it's your best bet.

························································

## GOING DOWN

My boyfriend has asked me if I will go down on him. I didn't understand so I said I would think about it. Could you please tell me what this means. I am seeing him the weekend after next and so would be obliged if you could reply in your column.

In the context in which your boyfriend uses it 'going down' means performing oral sex.

························································

## A REAL BASTARD

I don't know what to do. I work as a sales manager. My boss, who is a real bastard, seems to get a kick out of making life miserable for the people who work for him. He insists that we all work long hours but even though I've been working for him for eleven years I've never heard him say 'well done' or 'thank you' to anyone. The women in my office all complain that he touches them up at every available opportunity. And because he knows that the unemployed in my town stand a better chance of getting murdered than getting a job he behaves atrociously. He seems to get a special kick out of humiliating us all in front of one another. I'd love to give him a good thrashing but he knows damned well that I can't afford to lose my job. I have three teenage daughters and a wife and we have quite a good standard of living. None of them would be very pleased if I came home empty handed at the end of the month. My daughters are very status conscious and are constantly nagging me to buy my wife a better car. They say it's embarrassing to have to be picked up from school in a six-year-old car.

Your boss sounds the sort of person who starts the day with a raw liver sandwich, washes it down with a quart of rubbing alcohol and prepares himself for the day's work by watching old newsreel footage of Adolf Hitler practising the Berchtesgaden strut for his performances at the Berlin Odeon. He probably thinks that all this makes him a hard man. The truth is that people who behave the way that he does are usually riddled with self doubt and conscious of the fact that their shoe size is greater than their IQ. You can take some small comfort from the fact that underneath that harsh, uncaring exterior there lies a being with all the intelligence and the integrity of a suppurating ulcer. He's probably got a very small penis, too.

What's the worst that can happen if you stick up for yourself?

I'll tell you.

You'll lose a degrading, dispiriting, humiliating job that is destroying your soul and turning your life into a penance. And your wife and daughters will have to give up their charge cards.

What are you throwing your life away for?

If your family love you then they won't want you to stay in a job which is giving gangrene to your spirit. And if they don't love you—but just love the money you bring in—then stuff them.

Are you going to waste another 11 years of your life on this miserable job that is giving cancer to your self respect just so that your wife can have her nails buffed once a week and your daughters can ponce around in £90 trainers?

You'd be better off telling your boss what you think of him, buying yourself a ladder, a bicycle and a sponge and starting a window cleaning round.

While you're at it get the kids fixed up delivering papers.

## I LIKE TO FONDLE

I like to fondle my girl friend's breasts but some days she won't let me. I say that since we are living together I have a right to touch them whenever I want to but she says that I don't. I say that she says this because she has been listening to women's libbers. What do you say?

I say you big heap lump of stale boil oozings. What you say if your girlfriend say she have the right to squeeze your balls tightly every time she feels like it?

Has it occurred to you that the two lumps on your girl friend's chest are actually part of her body? Has it crossed your tiny, pimple sized mind that having your welding gloves kneading her tender bits may occasionally be painful?

No, I don't suppose it has.

Why don't you buy yourself a rugby ball, cut it into two and stick the two halves onto your string vest. That way you'll have a pair of breasts you can fondle all day long.

## INCURABLE PESSIMIST

I am an incurable pessimist. My boyfriend is always complaining because I am miserable but I cannot find very much in life to be happy about. Everywhere I look I see misery, cruelty and greed. I know I can't change the world but I would like to feel cheerful sometimes. Have you any advice you can give me?

Get a piece of paper and a pencil and write down as many details as you can remember of the seven happiest days of your life. (You must, surely, have had seven happy days in your life!) Next time you're feeling glum and overwhelmed by the horrors of the modern world escape into the memory of your seven happy days. The more you relive those memories the more realistic—and the clearer— they will become.

## SMALL NIPPLES

I have very small nipples. Is there anything I can take to make them larger?

A penis. If you get pregnant your nipples will probably increase in size.

## COMING BACK

What are you views on reincarnation? I recently visited a hypnotherapist who took me back to a previous life. During my very first session I learnt that in a previous existence I had been a French aristocrat. I was apparently beheaded during the Revolution. The hypnotherapist says this may be why I now suffer from frequent headaches. Do you agree?

Isn't it odd how everyone who can recall a previous exis- tence always claims to have been someone romantic and fascinating. I've lost count of the number of people I've met who used to be pirates, princesses, cavaliers or highly sought after courtesans. I'd be more impressed by theories of reincarnation if I heard from a few people who used to be bed-bugs, scrofulous chamber-maids or cholera ridden peas- ants. And why doesn't anyone ever remember dying in childhood? A few centuries ago infectious diseases meant that few children reached adulthood. Theories about reincarnation would stand up better if more supporters with good memories could only remember short and very miserable lives. You should ask your doctor to investigate your headaches. Modern X-ray apparatus will probably be more useful than a time machine.

......................................................................

## COCKEREL AND FAIRY

Last Friday my wife and I went to a party in fancy dress. I went as a cockerel and she went dressed as a fairy. During the course of the evening she spent a lot of time with someone dressed as the character Hotlips from the film M*A*S*H. At one point I saw them kissing and fondling one another. I didn't think much of it until quite late in the evening when I found out that the person dressed as Hotlips was in fact a man. I confronted them and flapped my wings to make it clear that I was not happy but my wife just laughed at me and carried on. What do you think I should do? My wife says that it was just innocent fun but when she got ready for bed I couldn't help noticing that the white tights she was wearing were very badly laddered while her bra and her other under-garment seemed to have disappeared completely. I know for a fact that the tights were quite expensive and I think I ought to say something though I wouldn't like to say anything out of turn or to make any unjustifiable assumptions.

I thought that this letter was a fake. But no one could have made up this stuff.

First, get rid of the Cock costume. Where's your sense of style? No one goes to fancy dress parties dressed as Cockerels any more.

Second, be firm. Tell your wife that if she wants new tights they'll have to come out of her housekeeping allowance.

Third, put a postcard in the corner shop window asking if anyone's seen your wife's bra and knickers.

Fourth, if you've ever done an assertiveness course ask for an immediate and full refund.

## DUE TO BE MARRIED

I am due to be married in July. But I have a very real worry. A few days ago I met my husband-to-be's former wife and she warned me that one of the reasons why she divorced him was the fact that he has such a large penis that sex with him was too painful for her to stand. My brother, who has seen my husband-to-be in the showers at the local swimming pool, has also warned me about what to expect on our honeymoon. I am now very nervous. I have been married before but my husband was not unusually well endowed and I have never had any sexual experience with anyone else. I have not had any children and I think that I myself am rather small down below. My husband-to-be and I have not made love yet and I am now getting very anxious about whether or not I will be able to cope.

I get long (and sometimes admirably graphic) letters like this every week. Either the world is full of petite women marrying well hung men or this is the most popular of all feminine fantasies. The fact is that you are extremely unlikely ever to find a man who is so well equipped that sex is impossible or unbearably painful.

## ONLY 18

My son wants to go away on holiday with two friends. He is only 18 and we think he is too young to go away by himself. What do you think?

Your son is old enough to vote, drink, drive, get married, become a father, take out a mortgage and die for his country. I think he's probably old enough to lie on a beach and turn brown without having his mum on hand to turn him over before he starts burning. If you're worried about him getting into trouble with girls you can comfort yourself with the knowledge that he can get into as much trouble in the car park at the local cinema as he can underneath the pier. Before he goes away warn him that he'll get piles if he sits on damp grass and remind him to change his underwear regularly. Then all you have to do is worry.

## OVER HIS KNEE

My husband and I had a steaming row the other evening. Eventually he got so cross that he picked me up, put me over his knee, pulled down my jeans and spanked my bottom. I was fighting as hard as I could but he is much taller and stronger than I am and I couldn't free myself. At first I felt humiliated and angry but much to my surprise I found that I became sexually aroused. He obviously did too and when he eventually stopped spanking me we had really good sex. Is there anything strange or unhealthy about this? I feel rather guilty about it but wouldn't mind trying it again sometime and don't know how to suggest it.

There isn't anything strange or unhealthy about it. They do it all the time in Belgium. If you want to try it again why not just try being deliberately naughty? And then when he looks at you sternly you can say (with wide open eyes, fluttering eyelashes and a feigned look of terror): 'Oh dear, you're not going to spank me again, are you?'

## TOLD OFF

My husband is an officer in the forces. I recently got told off (quite publicly) by a senior officer's wife after she had seen me eating an orange in the street. She made me feel very small and said that as an officer's wife I should behave like a lady at all times. My husband also got told off by his superior. He was furious with me.

It's good to know that the nation is in such safe hands. If the Chinese ever come over and start eating oranges in our streets they'll soon be made to feel really small. Being in the forces during peace-time isn't a proper job for anyone so I suppose that's why they get so terribly excited about the public consumption of fruit. Can't you persuade your husband to get a job in the real world and bring you back to reality? I've always thought that this archaic military fetish for 'proper' behaviour was a bit of a joke but if you're caught up on the edges of it then it can't be much fun.

## REAL POSER

My boyfriend is a real poser. I love him a lot but he is very vain and spends a fortune on clothes and sunbeds. He spends more on cosmetics and hairdressing than I do. How can I persuade him that these things don't matter? We want to get married but I can't see us ever being able to save up enough money if he keeps spending money this way.

As far as a man is concerned clothes should have three purposes: to keep out the cold, to prevent arrest for indecent exposure and to provide pockets to carry things in. Any man whose purchase of clothes is not primarily directed by these three basic instincts is either gay or foreign. Or both. Any man who spends time on a sunbed should be a worry to his mother.

## SLEPT TOGETHER

I am a single, male school teacher. Recently I took a group of children away on a trip to France. While we were away I became very friendly with another teacher, a woman in her late twenties who was divorced from her husband just three months ago. On our last night away we slept together for the first time. I was very surprised when we got into bed together. I am not very experienced sexually (this was only the second time I had been to bed with a woman) and some of the things the woman did quite shocked me. She told me that she liked being made love to while she was kneeling on all fours. I had always assumed that this was a position favoured only by animals. Do you think there is anything unusual or unnatural about her tastes?

No. Since, as you say, the position your friend finds most satisfying is one favoured by many animals it is clearly not unnatural. And it certainly isn't unusual. Lots of women find the 'rear entry' position particularly satisfying. Women who like to maintain an emotional distance during sex or who prefer to let their partner take control prefer this position—as do women who enjoy deep penetration. Incidentally, because it is a way of having sex without the two partners being able to see one another the rear entry position is particularly popular among Eskimos who favour it when lending their wives to visitors on dark, cold nights. Remember this little piece of sexual etiquette if you ever visit an igloo and get invited to stay the night.

## BOXING

Will you please support the campaign to ban boxing?

No. Boxing is a primitive, bloodthirsty and often unpleasant sport but it offers opportunities for boys who would otherwise have no hope. It provides an outlet for aggression and teaches boys about discipline etc. Most important of all, if boxing were made illegal it wouldn't stop—it would just go underground. And boxers would then be in even greater danger. I fear that those who want boxing banned just haven't thought things through. Anyway, if boxing is banned because it is dangerous to the participants we would also have to ban motor racing, skiing, rugby, football, yachting, swimming, drinking milk and watching television—all of which are probably more dangerous than boxing.

## TEENAGE DAUGHTERS

My two teenage daughters say that eating meat is cruel. They have both become vegetarians. They say that when animals are taken into an abattoir they must be frightened and that this means that the levels of adrenalin in their blood must increase. They've read somewhere that this increase in adrenalin levels could lead to illnesses such as high blood pressure and heart disease. Do you think that eating meat taken from dead animals could be dangerous? If not how do I persuade my daughters to start eating meat again. I am worried that they will become ill if they stick to a vegetarian diet.

It isn't just the amount of adrenalin in dead animals which worries me (though I do agree that this could cause problems). But what if a cow had a small cancer developing? I know animals are inspected but the inspections can't possibly be close enough to pick up small, developing cancers. This means that next time you sit down to tuck into a steak you might end up chewing a lump of cancer. Can you get cancer by eating it? I don't know. Nor, I suspect, does anyone else. There is no reason why your daughters should suffer ill health if they stick to a vegetarian diet. On the other hand, I believe that you are exposing yourself to a wide range of disorders by eating bits of dead animals.

## DIFFICULT POSITION

For twelve years I have worked for a small company but recently we were taken over by a large conglomerate which has many policies which I abhor. I find myself in a difficult position. Should I give up my job (knowing that it will be difficult to find another) or should I carry on?

The answer isn't as clear cut as you make out. You have suggested that you have only two choices: to stay or to leave. In fact there is a third choice. You can stay in your job and do whatever you can to try to change your company's policies. Organise petitions and protests. Write to the chairman. Put an open letter up on the notice board. The bigger the fuss you make the better your chances of changing things. You need only feel guilty about taking your company's money if you stay silent. If you make your voice heard you can hold your head up high. You may get the sack but you may be able to change things. Anyone too frightened of getting the sack to speak out is already dead in spirit.

## POSING NUDE

My boyfriend, who is a policeman, wants me to pose nude for photographs. He has found a magazine that will pay quite a lot of money for this sort of picture. I don't want to do it but he says that I would if I loved him. I am frightened that people I know will see the pictures. My boyfriend says I'm being selfish and silly because the money would be useful.

Anyone who tries to persuade someone else to do something they don't want to do by saying 'you would if you loved me' is a blackmailer of the very worst sort. Your boyfriend makes plankton look attractive. He should have a great future with the police. I suggest that you dump him and find yourself a nice, ethical bank robber. Or if you want a compromise tell him to take his clothes off and you'll take the photographs. Then sell the pictures to a gay magazine and send copies to all his friends.

## DAMNED MONEY

I won a considerable amount of money four months ago.

I tried to keep it quiet but the local newspaper found out and eventually there were quite a few stories about me in the papers. I vowed that the money wouldn't change my life and that I wouldn't give up my job or stop seeing any of my friends but things haven't worked out as well as I'd planned. Many of my former friends won't speak to me. If I'm generous to people and offer them money or try to buy them things they say they need, they say I'm being brash and showing off. If I don't give people money when they ask for it they accuse me of being mean. My new car was scratched twice while parked at work and I got so fed up of the snide remarks about my not needing to work and taking a job from someone who did need the money that in the end I gave up my job. I wish I hadn't won the damned money now because it has ruined my life. Why do people behave this way?

Jealousy is something many human beings are very good at. If someone wins a lot of money decent people congratulate them and say 'I hope I'm that lucky one day'. Miserable bastards tend to say 'Why didn't I win? It's not fair. I deserve it just as much as you do.'

Whether you like it or not your win has changed your life permanently. Not even giving away the money you won would change things now because even if you haven't changed, your friends' attitudes have changed. Sadly, I'm afraid you will just have to rebuild a new life for yourself with new friends who can accept you for what you are now.

........................................................

## SNIFFING GLUE

I was waiting for a bus recently when I saw a crowd of young boys sniffing glue. Why do young people do this?

Because they are angry, frustrated, bitter, frightened and alienated. And they have nothing to lose. I once remonstrated with a young man who was playing with a nasty looking knife and pointed out to him that by carrying a dangerous weapon he was making it more likely that he himself would be injured. 'Why should I care?' he demanded. 'I haven't got anything worth living for anyway.' I shuddered with horror when he said it but I couldn't answer him because in some ways he was right. Until society offers young people jobs, hope and some sort of future countless thousands of them will continue to wreak havoc on streets where they feel unwanted and in towns where they feel alien. And they will continue to damage their own health with no thought for the future.

Politicians don't seem to understand this at all. I remember reading a statement from a politician telling young kids not to sniff glue because it could be bad for them. It was a real 'pull up your socks and play the game' statement. He didn't seem to understand that there is something deeply wrong with a society in which 12-year-old children are so miserable, so lonely and so deprived of hope that they spend their free time huddled underneath canal bridges sniffing glue out of crisp bags so that they can escape from the world we have created for them.

......................................................................

## GOOD AT FOOTBALL

I am good at football and would love to take it up profes-sionally. I have been offered a job with a league club but I have also got a place at college to study engineering. My parents say that I should take the college place. They say that I can always play football when I've finished my course—but that I will at least have some qualifications behind me if things don't go well. What do you think?

When I was a kid I went out to tea with some relations. There were fancy cakes on a plate in the middle of the table and I was told that one of these was for me. I really looked forward to it. But being a good little chap I ate the rest of my tea first. When I got to the cake I was so full that I couldn't eat it. So I took the cake home with me to eat the next day. But the next day it was stale and tasted horrible.

If you put your opportunities on one side they won't always be there waiting for you when you decide you're ready. Your legs may have got slow by the time you've finished college. You may have developed arthritis or bunions. You may have had your leg broken in a bicycling accident.

If you give up the chance of a career in football you will always wonder whether or not you would have made it. And when you're old and wrinkly your grandchildren will get fed up of hearing you say 'I might have been a famous footballer, you know'.

By the time your three year college course is over you may be too old to take up professional football. The chances may no longer be there. Your natural skills may have faded. And once you've got a college qualification your parents will be even more reluctant to see you step off the career path to try out a life as a sportsman.

Why don't you ask the college to postpone your entrance for a year? Give yourself twelve months to see if you can make a go of a career as a professional footballer. Set yourself a target. For example, you might decide that if you haven't been offered a full contract or a first team place within twelve months then you'll take up the college place.

If you do choose to take your chances as a footballer, carry on with your academic studies at evening classes so that you don't get out of the habit of doing academic work. And remember that even if your football career doesn't work out, there is nothing to stop you going back to college as a mature student later. If you're a success and you make lots of money as a footballer, put aside a few quid so that you can afford to spend a year or two studying.

You only get one chance at life. And it is *your* life.

Never forget that death doesn't come at a convenient moment. The man with the scythe won't wait until you're ready and have tried out all your dreams. Life isn't fair or predictable. You have to take it by the scruff of the neck.

The real tragedy is that millions of people are dead at twenty. They just don't get buried for another half a century or so. They get carried on through life like driftwood, never taking control of their own destiny. 'Might have been' is the saddest phrase I know. Don't let your parents rule your life, because you are the one who has to live with your regrets.

........................................................

## TOO MUCH SEX

Can too much sex make you ill? My girl friend and I do it ten or twelve times a week—every night and most mornings. A friend I know said that if you have too much sex it can weaken your body and make you vulnerable to infection. Is this true?

Although I can't give you a definitive answer without knowing exactly how old you both are, how long you spend on sex and how exhausting each session is, I don't think you have too much to worry about—though you could find yourselves getting behind with your TV watching if you spend too much time screwing each other. You will undoubtedly be proud to know that I have put your names forward as contenders for places in my sponsored sex team at the next Olympics. (In case you've missed the news, it now seems possible that sex will eventually be accepted as a special event at the Olympics.)

Sexual athletes in all categories will be given points by six international judges. Points will be awarded for endurance, imagination, artistic performance, vocalisation and skill with a condom and so I would ask you to bear these things in mind during your sex sessions.

The sex team will meet at a secret venue for special training sessions every weekend from September onwards. No team coaches have yet been appointed.

........................................................

## SEX OBJECTS

My best girl friend won't settle down. She says she likes men as sex objects but hasn't yet found anyone she likes enough as a person to settle down with him. How can I persuade her that she is making a mistake? She is nearly 30 and isn't getting any younger. I've been married for six years and have a husband and two children!

Who says your girlfriend is making a mistake? I suspect that what you really mean is that while you have to walk round three supermarkets to find the nappies on special offer your girlfriend is spending her money on sexy new underwear, and while you worry about washing socks and cooking chips your girlfriend is busy working out which brain dead boyfriend to bonk next.

Stop trying to interfere and let your girlfriend enjoy herself. Indeed, why not relax a little and live your life vicariously through your friend. She has a long way to go yet. I know of one single woman who worked in a large office building who had a sign saying MEN put on her door in order to ensure that she received a constant and satisfactory supply of male partners. She boasted that every day strange men walked into her office unzipping their flies.

## IN HER UNDERWEAR
## (FIRST £1,000 CHALLENGE LETTER)

My wife is a member of a local drama society. A few months ago she appeared in a production in which she had to appear on stage in her underwear. She has a very good figure and was a real 'hit' with the audience. On the last night she bent forward and 'accidentally' fell out of her bra, which was one of those very flimsy ones, far too small for her breasts, and the men in the audience went wild. Afterwards a man approached her asking her to appear in a video he was making. He said it would involve her appearing nude with one other woman and two men but that he would pay her well. We talked about it and agreed that she should make the video since we needed the money to help with our mortgage payments. I think we both knew what the video would entail, though neither of us talked about it.

I have just seen the video and I was, I have to admit, very excited to watch my wife making love to complete strangers. The video was very professionally made and the director said he was very pleased with my wife's performance. He has asked her to make two more videos for him. The money is very attractive and since my wife is enthusiastic I have agreed. All actors and actresses in this director's films have to be screened in advance to ensure that they do not have any sexually transmitted diseases and I find this very reassuring.

I get so many letters describing bizarre sexual experiences that I've decided to introduce the Vernon Coleman £1,000 Challenge. You send me letters about your most bizarre sexual experiences—real or fantasy. Mark letters 'Challenge'. Each week I'll choose one and then say whether the letter is real or not. If you can prove me wrong I'll pay £1,000. This competition will continue either until I get fed up or I go broke. Incidentally, the letter above is quite definitely real.

## WHINING KIDS

My children dominate my life and I'm fed up of their constant demands and their never ending whining. I suppose I still love them (I don't have much time to think about things like love) but I certainly don't like them.

Maybe there was a mistake in the maternity ward and you've got the Munsters' kids. Or maybe you've got some wretched Royal leftovers.

Even if you got the right ones your feelings are not abnormal. It is, I'm afraid, quite natural for mothers (and fathers) to go through phases of disliking their kids. These feelings are inevitably accompanied by intense feelings of guilt. The best remedy is to find yourself a hobby or interest outside the home so that you can rebuild your shattered confidence and remind yourself that even parents have a right to a decent life.

## LADY FRIEND

I am 68 years old and I have a lady friend who is 20 years younger than me. We have sex at least once a week. I am beginning to worry that I may be doing myself harm. At what age should a man stop having sex?

You must stop having sex when they have nailed down the lid. This is the law.

## A WONDERFUL GIRL

I have fallen in love with a wonderful girl. I can't get her out of my mind. I dream about her at night and think about her all day long. I think she feels the same about me. My problem is that we haven't made love yet and I have an almost constant erection. Could this be harmful?

Constant excitement without release may damage your prostate gland so you should try to get rid of your erection occasionally.

There are several ways of doing this.

You could, for example, try thinking of any female politician or television presenter. That should swiftly and successfully eradicate any uncontrollable sexual urges.

Or you can use the time honoured auto erotic digitally controlled manual expression technique.

## DICKHEADS

What is the difference between a psychologist and a psychiatrist?

The daft answer is £30,000 a year, a car parking space and an index linked pension scheme. But that is completely unfair. There are huge differences. A psychologist studies behavioural patterns and tries to help patients suffering from mental disorders by understanding them. A psychiatrist is someone suffering from a severe personality disorder. Oh, no, whoops! Sorry. My mistake. That's a psychopath. Forget that. If there's time I'll try to get the sub editors to take that out so that I don't get sued. A psychiatrist tries to help patients either by giving them vast quantities of partly tested drugs or by pumping electricity into their brains. Most psychiatrists are complete dickheads.

·······················································

## SHOWING OFF

My boyfriend loves to show me off. He buys me very revealing clothes which I quite enjoy wearing and when the sun shines he gets me to strip off naked in the garden. I do get quite a thrill out of it and though the neighbours have not complained I do feel very naughty afterwards. My mum would have a fit if she knew that I was lying around nude. What do you think?

As long as you're both happy there is nothing to worry about. If the neighbours complain I can arrange to have them certified insane.

By the way you didn't give your full address. Please rectify this before the next warm spell.

·······················································

## LAZY NURSES

I recently had to spend ten days in hospital. The nurses were ignorant, callous and lazy. I feel that the days of long suffering 'angels' are long gone. Nurses work short hours and are paid well—with lots of perks. Quite frankly, none of them would last a day working in my office where the pressure is constant. I wish people would stop regarding nurses as something special.

You may have been unfortunate and the nurses who looked after you may have been guilty as charged. For heaven's sake make an official complaint so that other patients won't have to put up with less than perfect care. But if you think that your office job comes close to a nurse's job for real pressure you need to get Dr Frankenstein to tighten your neck bolts. How many times a day do you have to comfort people who are dying? How many times a day do you have to wash blood and shit off your hands? How many times a day do you have to struggle to keep another human being alive?

## CHARITY CLOTHES

Is it possible to catch any diseases after buying clothes from a charity shop?

Yes. For example, if you flew to Africa in your charity shop clothes you could catch malaria. Most charity shops clean the clothes they sell so your chances of catching something from the clothes themselves is slim.

## KISSING THE BRIDE

Where did the custom of male guests kissing the bride start?

In many countries it was for centuries the right of the local Lord, the clergyman performing the wedding ceremony or the monks from the nearest monastery to deflower the bride. But the traditional kiss from all male guests is probably all that is left of the custom which ruled that all the male guests were entitled and expected to make love to the bride before the groom.

Modern brides should think themselves lucky that all they have to put up with from Uncle Hector is a rather drunken peck on the cheek.

## HAPPILY ENGAGED

I am happily engaged to a girl I work with but on a fishing holiday with a group of mates I had a fling with a girl who won't stop bothering me with phone messages and letters. I haven't replied to any of her letters and I leave my phone machine on so that I don't have to speak to her but she now says that she's coming to see me. She says she wants to move in with me and that she has already given in her notice at work. How can I stop her coming? I don't think I bothered to tell her that I am engaged. If my fiancée finds out she will make my life miserable.

If it was just a 'fling' how did you come to give her your phone number and address? She clearly doesn't think of your relationship as merely a 'fling' and I doubt if you gave her the impression that you did when you were unzipping your trousers. For heaven's sake borrow the courage and be honest with her. I'm glad your fiancée is capable of making your life miserable. I hope you marry her, have three noisy, ungrateful and whining children and spend the next 30 years being slowly henpecked to death. You deserve it.

## TOO MANY NIPPLES

I have two nipples on one breast. Is this anything to worry about?

No. Supernumerary nipples (extra nipples) are fairly common. They are easy to remove. Go and see your doctor.

## ALWAYS LUMBERED

At work it's always me who gets lumbered with organising collections for people who are leaving or getting married. I'm secretary of our Wives Group, I do the laundry for my husband's football team and I'm secretary of my son's scout group. Why is it always me who gets the boring jobs?

Probably because you don't say 'No' often enough. Try saying 'No'. Practise it. Imagine yourself saying 'No' next time you're asked to do something you don't want to do. Be firm and don't ever give an excuse. If you say 'No, I can't do that because...' you'll probably still end up doing whatever it is that you don't want to do.

••••••••••••••••••••••••••••••••••••••••••••••••••••••••••••••

## WET HAIR

Does going out of the house with your hair wet increase your chances of catching a cold? My mum says it does.

No. Sorry, mum. Colds are caused by viruses which, although powerful, are too small and stupid to know whether or not your hair is wet.

••••••••••••••••••••••••••••••••••••••••••••••••••••••••••••••

## LIAR

My boyfriend tells lies all the time—even when there is no reason for it and nothing at stake. Is there anything I can do to change him?

As a general rule it is always a bad idea to try to persevere with a relationship on the grounds that you may be able to persuade someone to make a fundamental change in their personality. You're almost certain to be disappointed. Even if you talk to your boyfriend about his lying how will you know whether or not he's taken any notice of you? He's bound to say that he'll stop lying. But he'll probably be lying. If your boyfriend is a compulsive liar now then he'll probably always be a compulsive liar. Some people just have an aversion to the truth. He'll probably come out in a rash if he starts being honest. If you can love him despite that then that's fine. But don't expect to change him.

········································································

## ESCORT

I met a friend from school the other day. She was driving a brand new sports car and wearing very expensive clothes. I know she isn't married and so over lunch I asked her what she was doing for a living. She said she was a model but then got very coy when I asked her more specific questions. Eventually she admitted that she worked for an escort agency. She said she does sleep with some of the clients but only if she really likes them. She said that meant that she wasn't a prostitute. I told her that she was deceiving herself. She admitted that her clients sometimes give her extra money if she has sex with them. I told her that I didn't want to see her again. My husband says I was being unfair but I think he only said that because he's a man. What do you think?

Well, for a start I don't think you're much of a friend. I think that you're interfering, self satisfied, sanctimonious and puritanical. And I think that you're too quick to condemn and far too ready to look down your nose.

How well does your life stand up to close examination? Let's take a look at your job, for example.

Do you ever distort the facts when talking to customers or clients? Do you ever say that Mr So and So is in a meeting when you know damned well that he's playing carpet golf or pocket billiards? Do you ever use the firm's phone for private calls or take pens home with you? If you do any of these things then you're a liar or a thief. If you do them all then you're a liar *and* a thief. And if you don't have a job but depend on your husband for financial support your friend might claim that you are just an escort girl with one client.

Your friend sleeps with selected clients occasionally. They give her money. She presumably takes precautions to make sure that there are no unpleasant, long lasting consequences as a result of these temporary arrangements.

Who's hurt?

Compared to people in a lot of professions your friend is an angel.

Consider lawyers, for example.

They sell their minds and their integrity. When a client pays a lawyer a fee he buys the lawyer's intellectual skills. How many lawyers only represent clients who they like?

I'd rather have lunch with a prostitute than a lawyer.

Come to think of it I'd much rather have lunch with your friend than with you.

........................................................................................

## HORRID STEPCHILDREN

My stepchildren are really horrid to me. If I try to punish them they always point out that I am not their real mother. This usually makes me cry. As you can imagine my life is truly miserable.

Someone should rewrite those old stories in which wicked stepmothers played a crucial role. Wicked, manipulative, unscrupulous stepchildren are much more common than wicked step-parents.

Your husband, the children's father, has the key role in all this.

He should have a gentle word with his kids, tell them he loves you and gently explain to them their responsibilities and duties to you.

If that doesn't work he should threaten to stop them watching any television for a week. This is by far the most effective threat these days. There is no point at all in threatening to beat the shit out of them. The little bastards will simply call in the police. But most kids are so hooked on the magic lantern that they will do anything rather than risk a week of cathode ray tube deprivation. As far as I know it isn't yet illegal to stop kids watching television (though if dork brain social workers get their way it probably will be soon).

## PSYCHIATRISTS (AGAIN)

You recently said that most psychiatrists are complete dickheads. I think that was unfair.

You're right. I apologise. They're all complete dickheads. So are all lawyers, administrators and people who have little signs saying BABY ON BOARD or CHILD ON BOARD stuck on their car windows.

## DENTIST

My dentist wants to take out all my teeth. He says that it would take a lot of time to do all the necessary fillings and that it will be easier for me to have false teeth. He says that he might as well take out the few healthy teeth I've got while I'm under the anaesthetic. What do you think I should do?

Buy yourself a pair of running shoes so that if you see this dentist approaching you then you can run very quickly in the opposite direction. The man is a butcher. I don't suppose he's a rather elderly looking German, is he? If you do have the misfortune to see him again ask him if he used to be known by the name Mengele.

## ALTERNATIVE

I live abroad and suffer from a number of chronic ailments (including asthma, arthritis and eczema) and after several years unsuccessful treatment from orthodox doctors I am keen to try alternative medicine. I recently saw an advertisement for a local alternative health care practitioner who is fully qualified in osteopathy, homoeopathy, acupuncture, herbalism and hypnotherapy. He is apparently quite expensive but I am reassured by the fact that he has a number of impressive looking qualifications. What do you think?

By all means try an alternative medical practitioner. But ask around friends and relatives to find a practitioner you can trust. It takes years to obtain proper qualifications in the many different branches of alternative medicine and there are very few people under the age of ninety who are qualified in all the different disciplines you list in your letter. On the other hand it is possible to buy over-the-counter diplomas that sound far more significant than they really are, so it is important to be careful.

............................................................

## SMILING DOCTOR

After a routine medical examination my doctor told me that I was very healthy and that I would never have a stroke. When I asked him how he knew that he just smiled knowingly and said that doctors know these things. Do you know?

It's not as clever as your doctor would undoubtedly like you to imagine. I suspect that your doctor probably found that your blood pressure is quite low. Since strokes, heart attacks and other potentially deadly incidents are often caused by high blood pressure it stands to reason that people with low blood pressure are less likely to suffer from these problems.

............................................................

## EPILEPSY

I suffer from epilepsy and have to take pills every day. I have not had a fit for two years now but when I applied for a job with the local council I was told that I could not be employed because of my condition. The man who interviewed me said that the council's insurers will not allow them to employ people with epilepsy.

What a load of absolute crap. I have telephoned the Chief Executive of your local council. If you reapply your application will be favourably reconsidered. The idiot in the suit who told you this rubbish, whose IQ is clearly lower than his shoe size will, I hope, be given a black sack and a pointed stick and redeployed in the parks department.

••••••••••••••••••••••••••••••••••••••••••••••••••••••••••••••••

## INTERVIEW SUIT

I always wear the same suit when I go to interviews and as soon as I put it on I feel nervous. I recently put it on to go out to a function and I even felt nervous then! Do you think it is possible for some clothes to retain bad 'vibes'?

No, but it is possible for you subconsciously to learn to associate certain clothes with specific responses. I once had a suit (it long ago went to a charity shop) and every time I put it on I could feel my heart beating faster because I'd usually kept it for important meetings. For this reason it is a bad idea to have an 'interview outfit'. If you do then you'll always feel nervous when you're trying to be at your best.

Incidentally, this is the same phenomenon which explains why sports teams usually do better when they are playing at home where they have practised and why students are more likely to pass an examination if they take it in a classroom where they've done a good deal of their studying.

••••••••••••••••••••••••••••••••••••••••••••••••••••••••••••••••

## VIVISECTORS

Why do you hate vivisectors so much?

Because they are all nasty little psychopaths who deserve to be buried up to their necks in the fast lane of the nearest motorway.

## CONFERENCE (£1000 CHALLENGE LETTER)

My wife and I recently attended a conference at a large, luxury hotel. On the Saturday night everyone had quite a lot to drink as the firm I work for was celebrating some excellent sales figures. My wife went up to bed just after midnight, saying that she would leave the key in the door so that I could get into the room when I was ready. Most of the other wives went up with her. I stayed down in the bar with some guys I hadn't seen for some time. I went up to bed at about 2 am, found what I thought was our room and let myself in. What I didn't know was that I had got out of the lift on the wrong floor.

Everything was dark so rather than wake my wife I just got undressed and climbed into bed. I was feeling fairly fruity so I started to fondle what I thought was my wife's bottom. The owner of the bottom responded eagerly and we made love.

Only when the woman turned on the light to go to the bathroom afterwards did we both discover that we had made a mistake. The woman, whose husband was still down in the bar, was the wife of one of my colleagues. I apologised and left and made my way back to my own room.

Since that date I have been consumed by guilt. Do you think what I did counted as adultery?

Should I tell my wife?

What are you going to tell your wife—that you have a vivid imagination and a penchant for erotic fantasy? Come on, surely you can do better than this! This letter is about as real and as convincing as a political manifesto. If you can prove that this pathetic story is true I'll send you my personal cheque for £1,000.

## SHY

I have been courting a very shy man for six months. After the first three months we eventually made love at my instigation, and after a lot of coercion on my behalf. But after that we didn't do it again. I put this down to shyness and decided to let things take their own course for fear of scaring him off. The mere mention of sex had him stuttering and hastily changing the subject. Two weeks ago we went to a friend's party and stayed overnight. When we retired to the bedroom I thought 'Great! This is it! No excuses now!'. But my boyfriend broke down when I made advances towards him, saying he could not make love to me as he has an unsightly condition on the glans of his penis called balanitis. I asked him to show it and it was grotesque to say the least. Lots of red and yellow spots with pus flowing from them. We both just sat and wept. After talking to him I gather that he receives treatment at a local STD clinic. I have subsequently discovered what the letters STD stand for and I am frantic with worry. What is balanitis? Could I have caught it that one time we made love? It is now three months since we made love and I don't have any symptoms. What should I do? Where does it leave our relationship?

Balanitis can look a lot worse than it is. It's an inflammation of the glans or head of the penis and the surrounding foreskin. Symptoms include pain, itching and redness. Balanitis can be caused by all sorts of things—including infection—and the treatment inevitably depends upon the cause. If your boyfriend's balanitis was caused by an infection then you might have caught the same infection and you might, therefore, also need treatment even though you haven't noticed any symptoms. The treatment will probably involve a course of antibiotics.

Do remember, however, that balanitis is *not* necessarily sexually transmitted. Although your boyfriend may be getting treatment at an STD (sexually transmitted diseases) clinic, that might just be because the doctors there know more about sore and infected penises than anyone else. If your boyfriend is uncircumcised and his balanitis persists then he may need to lose his foreskin.

You ask where all this leaves your relationship.

The answer is simple: your boyfriend's balanitis shouldn't affect your relationship any more than any other temporary incapacity. Even if his balanitis was sexually transmitted that really shouldn't make any difference either—unless he swore to you that he was a virgin. Anyone who has sex can catch a sexually transmitted infection.

## SWEET TALKING

Is it true that medicines sometimes work better if people have faith in them? Do you think this explains why some very unlikely remedies seem to work well?

It's absolutely true. At least fifty per cent of the population who are ill would get better if they ate a green sweet every morning and a yellow sweet every evening and—and this is the key—had faith that the sweets would do the trick. Next time you're not feeling well try saying to yourself: 'My body is making itself well'. Say it six times every four hours. It certainly won't do you any harm. And it may help more than you'd imagine it possibly could.

## ORAL SEX

During the last three months I've started performing oral sex on my boyfriend. In the same period of time I've put on quite a bit of weight—nearly a stone. I always swallow his semen when he comes. Do you think the two could be related?

There are about 5 calories to a single emission, roughly the same as half a cherry. And there are 3,500 calories to a pound of fat. So you would have to swallow 700 emissions to put on a pound of extra weight. So that means that for you to put on a stone your boyfriend would have had to come in your mouth nearly 10,000 times in three months. That works out at approximately 111 ejaculations a day. If he has achieved this remarkable feat let me know and I'll get him a lucrative performing contract in Hamburg. If you're still worried, just remember that you don't have to swallow, though I'm told that having a spittoon in the bedroom is considered rather common in some circles.

## BUSINESS TRIP (£1000 CHALLENGE LETTER)

My husband was away on a business trip and I was feeling really miserable and lonely when a girlfriend of mine rang up unexpectedly. I hadn't seen her for years. When I told her that I was on my own she suggested that we went out for the evening, and had a meal and a drink and a chat about old times. We went to a restaurant I'd never been to before and then went on to a club. We got chatted up by quite a few blokes which was quite nice but although we both had a few smoochy dances we both behaved ourselves. When I took my friend back home she asked me in for a coffee and we carried on talking. By the time I looked at the clock again it was 3 am and my friend suggested that I stay the night. I didn't fancy the drive home at that time so I said 'yes'. She only has one bedroom so it meant sleeping together but I didn't think anything about it. My friend lent me a nightie, we both showered and got into bed. And then it happened. The light was hardly out when I felt this hand pushing my nightie up. I could feel my heart beating as though it was going to burst. When my friend started fondling my breast I honestly didn't know what to do. In the end I was so mixed up that I didn't do anything and my friend obviously took my silence as a green light. She gently pushed my nightie all the way up, ducked her head down under the covers and started kissing my breasts. I did things with her that night that I never even knew women did with one another. It quite obviously wasn't the first time my friend had had sex with a woman. When I left the following morning I told my friend that it had been very enjoyable but that I was happily married and had been heterosexual all my life and intended to stay that way. Do you think my story is true or false?

Your story is false. It's quite well done but you've made it up. And I'll send you a personal cheque for £1000 if you can prove it's true. It's the end of your story that gives you away, I'm afraid. If your encounter had been real you would have been confused and bewildered by it.

..........................................................

## TROUBLE

Aren't you afraid that by attacking the establishment and the big powerful drug companies so much you will get into serious trouble? My friend says that maybe they will even try to have you put away or even killed.

Thank you for your concern but I don't think there's any danger of that happ...

..........................................................

## TWINS

A few months ago when my husband's twin brother was thrown out of his home he came to stay with us. On our visitor's first night both men stayed out late. When he finally came to bed my husband woke me up and made passionate love to me. Early the next morning I woke up and realised that it was my brother in law and not my husband who was in bed with me. Later, while I pretended to be asleep, my brother in law left and my husband got into bed and had sex with me.
Since then this has been happening frequently. I can't say that I mind and even without the sex with my brother in law I am having far more sex than I got before he moved in. Should I tell them that I know what they are up to?

That depends largely upon whether or not you mind things changing. Because if you speak up then things will probably change.

When they know that you know what is going on they may both be very embarrassed. The result could be an instant and dramatic reduction in your nookie ration. Or they may suggest an escalation. And you could end up playing a highly erotic version of piggy in the middle.

Somehow, I get the impression that you rather like the present situation. So I suggest that (apart from the usual moaning and groaning at appropriate moments) you keep quiet.

(I assume, by the way, that you are aware of the emotional and physical dangers of sharing your favours in this way.)

........................................................................................

## A CHANCE

I have been offered a chance to go round the world with two friends. I really want to go. I want to campaign for the environment and do something to stop all the pollution and so on and I think this is a good opportunity for me to find out exactly what is going on in different countries. Half the time my mum and dad say that I because I'm only 20 I'm too young to go. The rest of the time they say I should settle down and that if I go off round the world now there won't be any jobs available when I get back.

Mums and dads worry. That's why they sometimes forget to think before they speak. Hands up all parents who have said: 'Why can't you be like the other kids?' and then quickly followed it up with 'Do you have to do it just because everyone else do it?'

Most men and women start their lives feeling angry, full of fire and determined to change the world but they forget their dreams and save up for a tumble drier instead. Millions of people go through their teens full of enthusiasm and driven by a genuine desire to make the world a better place; happier and healthier for humans and animals. But most people are carried through life like pollen on the wind.

Talk to your parents. If you really, passionately believe that you should go then—if they truly love you—they will listen. If they still say 'no' then you have to decide whether to let them rule your life or to take control.

Just remember that in forty years time your regrets will tell you more about yourself—and the way you have lived your life—than your accomplishments.

• • • • • • • • • • • • • • • • • • • • • • • • • • • • • • • • • • • • • • • • • • • • •

## PARENTS

My parents are living alone and desperately need help and support. My brother and I do everything we can but it's not enough. We asked the local social workers to help but we got told, quite rudely, that there was nothing that could be done.

I have it on the strictest authority that by law all social work departments have to set personality and IQ tests for prospective employees. There is, however, a small snag. The national computer programme which organises the tests was set up upside down and back to front. As a result the only social workers who are ever hired are the ones who have failed all the personality and IQ tests. I telephoned your local office and spoke to a remarkable sequence of blancmange brained morons. I eventually got through to the one fellow in the office who seems to have been born with a complete brain. Telephone tomorrow morning and mention my name. I suspect they may remember our conversation and be able to help you.

• • • • • • • • • • • • • • • • • • • • • • • • • • • • • • • • • • • • • • • • • • • • •

## LOVE

My boyfriend says he loves me but I'm not sure. He only seems to say it when he wants me to make love to him. How can I be sure that he loves me?

You'll know he really loves you when he tells you that he loves you after you've made love.

.........................................................................

## RECORD

I am 18 and my girlfriend and I have made love at least
3 times a week for a year. Do you think this is a record?

I'm really fed up of people writing to me and boasting
about their sexual exploits (particularly when they are so
puny). What on earth makes you think I'm interested?
Three times a week wouldn't get you into the record books
for 80-year-olds—let alone 18-year-olds.

Here's a *real* sexual statistic. Let us assume that there
are 20 million couples within two hundred miles of where
you live who are capable of sex. If we assume that half of
those do it twice a week (and the rest don't do it at all) that
makes a total of 20 million sexual encounters every seven
days. If we assume that the average act of intercourse lasts
3.5 minutes and that the average number of in and out
movements per minute is 15, then the average number of in
and out movements per act of intercourse is around 50.

Since the average penis is six inches long all this means
that each act of intercourse produces around 300 inches of
penile movement.

If you're still with me you'll remember that I've already
established that there are 20 million sexual encounters a
week in your part of the world.

So we now multiply 300 by 20 million to get the total
number of inches of penile movement.

And we then divide 6000 million by 12 x 3 x 1760 x 7 x 24
to get the total number of miles of penile movement per hour.

To save you the trouble of finding your calculator the
answer is 564.

So, every hour, there are 546 miles of intra vaginal penile
movement.

*That* must surely be the most pointless, stupid and
totally useless piece of statistical information you are ever
likely to read anywhere.

So, remember: you read it here first.

## FLOPPY

I am 66 years old and my problem is that I don't find my wife attractive any more. She weighs twice what she did when I married her and has very pendulous and floppy breasts. Her size and shape do not turn me on at all and I have great difficulty in obtaining an erection on the rare occasions when we try to make love. I think I could be turned on by a slim, small breasted 20-year-old.

The $64,000 question is 'Would a slim, small breasted 20-year-old be turned on by you?'

Or are you, perhaps, showing some signs of increasing age and might you, in turn, prove to be something of a turn off for a younger and more attractive woman?

There is no law that says that you have to think about your wife when you are making love to her. The thought police haven't entirely taken over our lives—yet.

Don't be shy or embarrassed. Most men and women fantasise occasionally when making love.

Sometimes the fantasies involve the same partner but different circumstances. (Some couples actually share their fantasies with one another.) And sometimes the fantasies involve an entirely different partner.

You will, I suspect, find that adding excitement to your sex life by using your imagination will be far less expensive, far less traumatic, far less injurious to your health (and—if you're a celebrity—far less likely to put you on the front page) than trying to add excitement by straying away from home.

## AFFAIR

My wife has been having an affair for nine months. She lets her lover bring her home every evening and they kiss very passionately in his car outside. I have tried threatening her but she just tells me how good he is in bed and that he can he satisfy her whereas I cannot.

If you've tried talking and got nowhere, there are two things you can do.

First, you could suggest that the pair of you go and see a counsellor together. If that suggestion falls on stony ground—and your wife refuses to go with you—then you could try issuing an ultimatum.

If you tell your wife that she must choose between you and her fancy man, and you make it clear that you mean business, then everything will be brought to a head. Give her a week to think it through.

If you do this then you may lose your wife. But do you really want to keep her under the present circumstances? It sounds a pretty miserable way to live to me.

## FLIRT

My husband is a terrible flirt. At parties he always stares at pretty women and during the summer he is a positive menace while out driving because every time he sees a girl in a short skirt or a low cut sleeveless top he stares and stares and stares. He even flirts with our baby sitter who is only 18 years old.

You'd have more to worry about if he didn't flirt and didn't stare at pretty women. Men who spend hours staring at women rarely do much serious frolicking, just as women who spend hours looking in shop windows rarely do much serious shopping. You should start worrying seriously when your husband deliberately averts his eyes when tempted by a flash of creamy white thigh or a provocative hint of awe inspiring cleavage.

Any man who doesn't look at pretty girls in short skirts is either gay or a guilt stricken adulterer struggling hard to persuade his wife that he is neither guilt stricken nor an adulterer.

........................................................

## STALE

My marriage has become rather stale. I want to liven it up
a little. In the morning when my husband says goodbye to
me I'm usually wearing a housecoat and I never even have
time to do my hair. In the evening, when he gets home, I'm
surrounded by kids and I know I smell of baby food,
washing powder and chips. How can I grab his attention?
I talked to a friend about this and she said she'd have the
children so that I could strip naked and meet him at the
door with a bottle of wine in one hand and two glasses in
the other. It's an exciting thought but I think that might be
going a bit too far. What do you think?

I don't recommend meeting your husband naked. For one
thing he might bring the boss home with him. And you
might feel a bit silly if you opened the front door and found
the vicar standing there. I can just hear you. 'Oh, hello,
vicar! I was in the bath. I thought you were the blind piano
tuner.'

(Mention of a blind piano tuner reminds me of a true
story. A pal of mine who is a piano tuner was standing in for
a blind colleague. He turned up at a large house and was
met by an attractive, well built woman in her forties. She
was doing her housework absolutely stark naked and had
obviously assumed that all piano tuners are blind. My pal
says that he immediately realised that to avoid any embarrassment he would have to pretend to be what is, I believe,
now known as visually grossly impaired (translated into
English this means 'blind as a bat'). So he stumbled into the
house and let the woman take him by the arm and lead him
to the piano. Everything went well—and the woman carried
on doing her dusting in the nude—until my pal needed to go
to the loo. Again the woman led him there by the arm. When
he came out he forgot to pretend to be blind and made some
comment about a picture the woman had got hanging on the
wall in her loo. My pal says he'd never seen a woman go so
completely red or run upstairs quite so quickly).

On the whole, I think a more subtle approach might be both safer and more effective.

One of the strange things about life is that we invariably find things much more exciting if there is an element of mystery to them. Wrapped packages are more intriguing than unwrapped ones.

There were two pretty women walking along the street in my nearest town the other day. The blonde wore a skirt that came down to two inches above her knees. The brunette wore a skirt that came down to several inches below her knees but had a slit up to two inches above her knee. The brunette's skirt gave passers by no more than a glimpse of what the blonde's skirt gave without any effort. But the brunette's skirt was far more sexually provocative and attractive. The unknown, the hidden and the hinted at are always more exciting than the obvious and the blatant.

Buy yourself some sexy underwear and some sexy clothes and make sure you find the time to wear them.

......................................................

## SAVING

My boyfriend and I are saving up to buy our own house but it is slow going. My boyfriend says that he can get me a job working in a topless bar. He says it's harmless enough and will bring us in quite a lot of money. Do you think I should do it?

No. Your boyfriend sounds as if he's an aspiring pimp. Unless *you* want to work in a topless bar tell him to get lost. Taking off your clothes professionally is a career choice that you—and you alone—should make.

......................................................

## OTHER WOMEN

My wife recently confessed to me that she has sexual feelings for other women. She says there is no one in particular that she wants to make love to but admits that she does have a general desire to have a sexual relationship with a woman. Our sex life is very good and varied. After a long discussion with her I said I understand and agreed that my wife could realise her desires if she wanted to. I don't feel threatened in the same way as I would if she wanted to see another man. Do you think this could cause any problems that I haven't already thought of?

It is a curious fact that large numbers of men feel the same way as you do. Many men who would become speechless, indignant, incoherent, tearful, whining, protesting wrecks at the prospect of their wives having sexual affairs with strange men greet the prospect of their wives having sexual affairs with strange women with comparative equanimity. Indeed, some men find the very idea of lesbianism so attractive that they get quite excited when their wives talk about having sex with another woman. ('Er, do you mind if I watch?')

Curiously, however, and in contrast, most women are likely to regard the idea of their male partner having a sexual relationship with another male as even more threatening and upsetting than him having a sexual relationship with another woman. This may be because whereas they can understand and compete with a female rival a male rival is less comprehensible. If you doubt this try suggesting to your wife that you might start having sex with men and see what she says. (These days the added hazard of AIDS— rather more likely to affect male than female homosexuals —undoubtedly complicates the picture).

What you have to remember is that whether she chooses a male or female lover the physical aspect of any affair your wife might have is less likely to prove damaging to your relationship than any emotional complications which might ensue. It is the emotional aspect of an affair which is most likely to wreak havoc with your marriage.

And I suspect that your wife is just as likely to become emotionally attached to a lover without a penis as she is to a lover with one.

So think about that.

How would you feel about your wife falling in love with another woman—and leaving your bed and home for hers?

························································

## HAIRY

I am 35, female and single and my life is not worth living. In recent years I have started to get hairier and hairier. I now have to shave my thighs as well as my legs and I have tufts of dark hair on toes and fingers. But the worst is my face. I have thick dark hairs sprouting out all over my face. I have also put on a large amount of weight in recent months. My periods have stopped. Do you think I could be changing sex?

No, but there are other explanations. For example, you might have a condition called polycystic ovary (also known as Stein-Leventhal syndrome) which is caused by an imbalance in your hormones. If you do have this disorder it should be possible to treat it with hormones—or maybe with an operation. Whatever is wrong with you, my advice is that you should see your doctor and ask for him to arrange for you to see a hospital specialist.

························································

## THE WORLD

I sometimes get quite depressed about the world we live in. There is so much corruption and so much dishonesty in high places.

You aren't alone. The main trouble with this world is that someone put the grown ups in charge.

Most people who choose to become politicians, lawyers and establishment figures are ego laden megalomaniacs, quite blind to such economically unnecessary intangibles as passion and justice. The honest, the passionate and the genuinely well intentioned tend to be too naive and unworldly to succeed in any of these areas.

By the time they've licked enough bums to become government ministers and judges these professional grown ups are embittered and senile. The result is that they screw things up and make decisions which no sensible citizen can understand. I honestly doubt if there is a judge or government minister who could hold down an ordinary, responsible job for more than half a week. Most of them could win gold medals for their stupidity. They could be stupid for their country.

That's why the world is an unpalatable mess.

But if you don't like it and you want to change it there are a lot of things you can do.

For example, if you really want to do something then try writing one angry letter a day telling politicians why they are making a mess of running the country. You'll make your voice heard, you'll feel better and you'll be doing your bit to change things. If the millions of readers of this column who genuinely care about the world all wrote one angry letter a day to their political representative or some other establishment figure then the world would change.

The world is a dishonest and depressing place—run by mean spirited, passionless grown ups—because too many of you don't have faith that you can change things.

Trust me. You can.

........................................................

## DOLLY BLUE

Could you please tell me where I can buy dolly blue. I have asked at all the supermarkets and hardware shops and had no luck. It is used for getting white shirts whiter.

Start at the bus station, go past the old church and down the hill. Pass the car park and turn first left and then first right underneath the railway bridge at the bottom of the hill. There's a shop on the corner called Alf's Mini Mart.

(Seriously, why do people send me letters like this? I must have the oddest mailbag in the world. Why on earth does someone think I know who sells dolly blue? I don't even know what the damned stuff is. And please don't write and tell me.)

........................................................

## COLD WATER

Could you please tell me the benefits to be obtained from the practice of spraying warm and cold water on one's testicles and penis daily.

If you keep doing this for another thirty years you may eventually realise what an absolute plonker you've been and how much of your life you have wasted. If you spend just five minutes a day doing this then in 30 years time you will have wasted 912 hours causing yourself discomfort and making a mess all over the bathroom for no obvious reason. Spraying your testicles with warm and cold water is such a perfectly pointless activity that it would come as no surprise to me to hear that politicians (the male ones at least) were all doing it twice a day. It could well be made into a law.

In answer to your question I don't think there are any benefits as far as you are concerned but your letter gave the rest of us a giggle so thanks for writing in.

........................................................

## SMALL PENIS

I think the secret of a happy life is to find a partner who likes you the way you are and then relax. My penis is about three inches long but if a woman doesn't like it she can sod off.

Thank you for sharing this with us. Actually, although you have chosen a simple way in which to express a complex series of philosophical thoughts, I think you're absolutely spot on. Psychiatrists, psychotherapists and marriage guidance counsellors would all be out of work if everyone had these two sentences tattooed on their fore-heads at birth. Oh, all right, I'm exaggerating but you know what I mean.

·····································

## No GRATITUDE

Twice a week I fetch shopping for an elderly woman who lives near me. But she never says 'thank you' or expresses any gratitude. I don't mind doing things for her but it would be nice if, just occasionally, she said something.

Why? Isn't knowing that you're doing a kind deed enough? The old lady whose shopping you do is undoubtedly rather rude not to say 'thank you' occasionally but are you doing things for her because you want to help her or because you want her to be grateful? Think about it.

·····································

## NONSENSE

My husband had a vasectomy a couple of years ago. Afterwards he told me that he had been instructed that we had to have sex at least four times every week and when-ever he had the urge. Is this really true? I have done as he said because I didn't want his health to be put at risk but when I visited my own doctor complaining of soreness and exhaustion he said that what my husband had said was nonsense. What do you think?

I think you've been had. A lot.

·····································

## ANOTHER ESCORT

I read your recent letter about a woman who met up with an old friend who was working as an escort girl with special interest. I started working as an escort about a year ago. I regularly earn £2,000 a week and it is wonderful to be so independent. For the first time in my life I can afford to do what I want. I am totally in charge of my life and I love it.

All female politicians should be retrained to work in your profession. At the moment they spend their lives screwing the rest of us. The change would be nice for them.

......................................................

## CHRISTIAN

I thought your reply to that letter about the prostitute woman was disgusting. I am a Christian and women like that bring shame on us all.

I suppose you'd like to see all prostitutes tied up and stoned. It's good to know that the modern, evangelical spirit of Christian warmth, forgiveness and compassion is alive and kicking. May I suggest that you get hold of a copy of a book called The Bible? You might learn something from it.

......................................................

## PARTY

About five years ago I went to a party at a friend's house. Somehow we started talking about children being sexually abused by their fathers. For some reason I told my friends that I had been sexually abused by my father. I suppose I said it to shock them but it wasn't true. I now can't face my dad for the guilt I feel. Neither of the friends I told mentioned what I told them until recently when one suddenly asked me why I allowed my dad to babysit for my children after what he did to me. I was so shocked I didn't know what to say. We had a house full of people at the time. I didn't say anything but just tried to change the subject. I have tried to bring myself to tell the truth but I don't know what to say. I can't believe that anyone could make up anything so terrible. I feel like running away. I know I deserve to be unhappy but what can I do?

You must tell your friends the truth. It was an absolutely terrible lie which could get your father into awful trouble. Do whatever you have to do to convince those to whom you told this stupid story that you were lying.

.......................................................................

## CONSTANT ERECTIONS

My wife has always been an enthusiastic nudist and now wants me to join her club but I have constant erections when I think about going there—I hate to think what would happen if I actually went there. Is there anything medical I could take to stop me being aroused?

I can think of dozens of drugs that would stop you being aroused. The snag is that most of them would probably also stop you breathing and make your hair fall out. To be honest I don't think you need worry. You may think that you would find a visit to a nudist colony irresistibly stimulating but I doubt if the sight of 55-year-old naked women playing ping pong would provoke autonomic verticalisation of your fertilisation equipment. (Sorry about that. The euphemistic phrase is there because the Editor says I can't use the words 'penis' or 'erection' in case I offend the Good Christian Parents again. Whoops. I have. Now I'll probably get fired. Will you miss me?)

.......................................................................

## BABY WANTED

My husband and I would like to have a baby but so far we have not been successful. My husband says that he doesn't mind if I make love to someone else in an attempt to get pregnant. He has even suggested one or two men who he thinks might be suitable. Do you think this would be a sensible thing to do?

No. I think it would be a totally disastrous thing to do. Let's assume for a moment that it is your husband who is infertile and your entirely authorised evening of adultery leads to conception, pregnancy and childbirth. Imagine too that your husband can come to terms with the fact that the presence of your child is a constant, ever present reminder of your sanctioned infidelity. Now move on a few months. You and your lovely blond haired husband are playing with your cuddly little red haired baby. The child suddenly decides to do something horrible like throw a toy car through the TV screen or crap on the carpet. Can't you see what will come next?

'It's not my damned kid, anyway!' will become a refrain which will drive a stake through your marriage.

## PENIS ENLARGEMENT

Is it true that it is possible to have an operation for lengthening the penis? I am rather small in that department.

I love the way you describe yourself as being 'rather small in that department'. I have a vision of you being a trifle undersized in haberdashery but well endowed in household fabrics.

Surgeons in China and South Africa are now performing surgery which is said to extend the length of an average penis by 4 to 7 cm. But having a big penis won't guarantee you an earth shaking sex life.

## LOUD MUSIC

I go to discos two or three times a week. Is it true that listening to loud music can damage your hearing?

Yes. I said, YES!

## SMALL BUST

My bust is quite small (34B) and I am thinking of having surgery to make it bigger. My boyfriend is always telling me that he wishes my breasts were bigger. Do you think the operation being done now is safe?

Politicians and doctors will tell you that breast implants are safe but then who trusts politicians or doctors about anything? You could summarise what the current bunch of dickheads know about medicine, science and health care on the back of an atom with a five inch paint brush. I have no idea at all whether breast implantation is safe. And I doubt if anyone else has either. Buy yourself an uplift bra and a couple of handfuls of cotton wool. Or find a more gallant boyfriend who likes you the way you are.

## FEMININE CLOTHES

I am a 27-year-old male. From my early teens I have gradually collected a feminine wardrobe. All my leisure hours I think and live as a woman. I lie in bed in my sexy lingerie and play with myself until I get an orgasm. Should I consult my doctor?

I can think of no reason why you should consult your doctor about your peccadillo unless you think that he or she is likely to want to share your lingerie collection.

## ANTIBIOTICS

When my daughter had a chest infection her doctor gave her antibiotics to take for ten days but when I had a chest infection my doctor gave me the same pills for just five days. Can you explain why?

No one has yet decided whether antibiotics should be given for 5, 7 or 10 days. So some doctors prescribe them for 5 days. Some for 7 days. And some for 10 days. You may think that this displays a lamentable level of professional competence by doctors and a gross contempt for their customers by the pharmaceutical industry. If you thought this I would find it difficult to argue with you.

························································

## SOLIDS

At what age should I start my baby on solids? I am breast feeding at the moment and everyone seems to say something different. My friend says I should wean him off milk at 3 months. The midwife says 6 months and my mother says a year. My doctor says it's up to me.

Experts now seem to agree that the longer you can breast feed your baby the better. Having said that I must quickly point out that there are some limitations. For example, it is considered socially unacceptable in some quarters to continue to breast feed your son when he's captain of the school rugby XV. Not long ago I did hear of a woman who was still breast feeding her 14-year-old son. The expert view seems to be that babies should be breast fed until they are one-year-old.

························································

## LOVELY MAN

I have fallen in love with a lovely man. He is the kindest and most thoughtful man I have ever been with and I know he loves me. He is very gentle and is a considerate lover. There is only one problem. His penis is much smaller than anything I have encountered in the past and I find it impossible to obtain full satisfaction when we make love.

You can make more satisfying use of your partner's diminutive organ by careful selection of the positions you use while making love. Experiment and enjoy.

## CASUALTY

After a recent accident I had to go into the casualty department of my local hospital. I was amazed at the number of forms that had to be filled in. There were only two nurses on duty but there were three women in white coats handing out forms. I was in quite a lot of pain with a suspected broken arm and made a mistake on my forms. Despite my pain one of the white coated women made me fill in a completely new form before they would accept me for treatment.

I'm surprised that you were amazed. I thought it was common knowledge that health care had been taken over by administrators years ago. Hospitals used to be infested with cockroaches. These days the problem is administrators. Thousands and thousands of them; nasty, little creatures living in thickly carpeted offices. Not that it is only hospitals which are contaminated with administrators and bureaucrats. It sometimes seems to me as if the whole world has been taken over by these damned besuited lunatics. Most of them have a distorted sense of logic which defies all common sense.

A few days ago, for example, a polite and apparently quite sane young woman knocked on my door. She introduced herself as a health and safety officer of some kind and asked me if I was a farmer. I told her I wasn't. She then asked for my name. I asked her why she wanted to know. She said that since I wasn't a farmer 'they' needed my name so that they could take it off their records. I asked her why they needed my name in order to take it off their records if they didn't already have my name. I gently pointed out that the fact that they didn't have my name on their list seemed to suggest that I wasn't on their records and therefore didn't need to be erased. The young woman said they couldn't take me off their records unless I was on them and so they would need to know my name so that they could put it on and then take it off. She was quietly but firmly insistent and didn't seem to think that there was anything odd in what she was saying. I said goodbye and shut the door very quietly.

I have a strong suspicion that all administrators and bureaucrats are aliens from the planet Zog sent over here to try to drive the rest of us crazy. If we mistreat them, there has to be a chance that one day they will all go back home to Zog.

•••••••••••••••••••••••••••••••••••••••••••••••••••••••••••••••

## SHAKING HANDS

Is it possible to catch AIDS by shaking hands with a someone who has got the disease?

Yes. If you both have open wounds or cuts you could catch it by shaking hands. Other unusual ways to die include being hit on the head by ice falling from an aeroplane and strangling yourself by getting your tie caught in your car window and then slamming the door.

•••••••••••••••••••••••••••••••••••••••••••••••••••••••••••••••

## BAD EGG

My daughter has begun a relationship with a man whom I know is a real bad egg. I know he's a bad sort because I had an affair with him about two years ago and he dumped me. How can I warn my daughter about the sort of man he is without telling her how I know?

Unless you lie and say that you know he treated a 'friend' of yours badly you can't. And you should think carefully about your motives. Are you trying to protect your daughter, protect yourself or get a little revenge on your erstwhile lover? If you tell your daughter not to see this man you will have to explain why. And your daughter will probably suspect that you are acting through jealousy or spite. You and I both know that your motives are entirely honourable but will she believe you?

## BORING JOB

I have a very boring job with a plumbing supplies merchant but can see no way out. I am married with two young children and even though I'm not paid particularly well I need the money. When I stop to think about things I get very depressed. The idea of spending the next 30 or 40 years counting ballcocks and lavatory cisterns fills me with despair.

I'm not surprised. It would fill me with despair too. No sixteen-year-old dreams about counting ballcocks, selling sanitary towels or working for the council when he or she grows up. But most people do end up doing boring, mundane jobs. Not everyone can be a racing driver or a disc jockey.

I'm not going to try to make you feel important by giving you any garbage about the world needing lavatory cisterns because there isn't anything I or anyone else can say that will disguise the fact that you have a pretty crappy job.

There is, however, a very simple way in which you can acquire more self respect and get more fun out of your life: find yourself a captivating hobby or interest and then throw yourself into it with your whole heart.

Become an expert on fungi. Campaign for something you believe in. Stand for the council. Take up weightlifting, painting or growing miniature trees.

Your job may be dull but if you spend 40 hours a week at work (earning enough to keep you and your family in basic comfort) and 56 hours a week sleeping that still leaves you 72 hours a week to do things that you find challenging, exciting and rewarding.

## GIRLIE MAGAZINE

I recently found a copy of a girlie magazine in my husband's briefcase. It was full of pictures of big breasted women with no clothes on. What should I do? I am seriously thinking about leaving him. I was very shocked.

Funnily enough, girlie magazines usually are full of pictures of big breasted women with no clothes on. I'm told that the editor of one magazine tried replacing the photos of large breasted women with advice on putting up shelves and cutting wet grass but found that sales suffered noticeably.

My advice is that you put the magazine back exactly where you found it and give yourself a sharp slap across the wrist for being too bloody nosey for your own good. What were you doing looking in your husband's briefcase? If your husband had felt that you were broad minded enough to cope with his titillating magazine he would have presumably shown you the damned thing instead of hiding it away like an embarrassed schoolboy.

If you want to bring a smile to your husband's face you could try putting a tit magazine in his Christmas stocking, thereby both giving him a thrill and letting him know that you aren't quite as straight laced as he fears you are.

However, if you are as pompous and as bigoted as he clearly suspects (and your letter to me suggests that you may be) then perhaps you should do your husband a favour and leave him.

He can then get on with having a bit of fun and you can knit woolly squares for refugees.

••••••••••••••••••••••••••••••••••••••••••••••••••••••••••••••••

## GOD

I strongly object to your articles attacking scientists who perform animal experiments. Animals were put on earth by God so that man could use them.

I can sum up everything I wish to say to you in just two words. The second word is 'off'. I doubt if you are intelligent enough to guess the other word without any help so here is a clue: it is a four letter word which rhymes with 'luck' and starts with the sixth letter in the alphabet. You should get the answer by tea time on Wednesday.

## SINGLE STRIPPER

I am a single mother and I supplement my income by stripping in a pub on Sunday lunchtimes. Last Saturday evening my boyfriend made love to me on the carpet in my living room. When I went to work the following day one of the other girls pointed out that I had 'carpet burns' all over my back and bum. I had to do my whole act without turning round. The pub landlord wasn't very pleased because quite a few of his customers like seeing the girls' bottoms. Can you give me some advice for the future please?

This has got to be the oddest letter I've had since the one I received from a reader who wanted to know where she could buy something called dolly blue. In future I suggest that you enjoy your Saturday evening nookie on your knees. I doubt if any discerning member of a strip show audience would notice your knees if you painted them bright green with yellow spots on so carpet burns will go quite unnoticed.

## NERVY ATTACKS

I was put on tranquillisers thirty years ago because I was suffering a lot from stress. I came off them three years ago. I still get nervy attacks. Do you think these could be withdrawal symptoms?

No, I don't think so. Don't forget that you were originally given tranquillisers because you were having some sort of nerve trouble. The tranquillisers won't have cured you. Maybe you now need to learn to deal with your stress and anxiety more effectively.

## A THREAT

Your recently reported comments about solicitors screwing up people's lives were quite unjustified. My son is a solicitor and trained very hard to become one. If you write anything rude about solicitors again I will suggest that he sues you. It is libellous to say what you did. Solicitors are conscientious, sensitive people who do a great deal for the community. You can't say rude things about solicitors because if you do they will sue you.

If Attila the Hun came back for a second chance he'd come back as a solicitor. Dr Mengele would have been a solicitor but they threw him out of college for being too nice. If all the greedy, grasping, unsympathetic solicitors who are empty of social virtue were rounded up, they'd need a corral the size of the Arctic. Come to think of it, that would be a good place to send them. In one short letter you threatened to sue me twice. So sue me.

## THUNDERSTORMS

I am terrified of thunderstorms and absolutely hate going out in storms. The last time there was a storm I had to go out to collect the children from and I was sweating and shaking by the time I got there. Where can I get help?

Visit your doctor and ask him to arrange for you to see a psychologist (not a psychiatrist). He should be able to help you conquer your fear.

## TELEPHONE LOVE

I have fallen in love with a girl I have never met. I was feeling rather lonely recently so I telephoned one of those telephone lines where you get to speak to a girl on a one to one basis. She has a wonderful voice and I know she must be beautiful. She sounds around 20 years old—which is my age. I am desperate to meet her but she won't see me. How can I persuade her that I am genuinely in love?

Tell her that you know that she is 85 years old, wears a darned grey cardigan and sits doing her knitting while talking to you. Then she may agree to meet you. You have fallen in love with a fantasy, my friend. Forget it. The woman you think you love does not exist. Beautiful, buxom 20-year-olds do not sit on the other end of the phone talking to stray callers. Coleman's 57th Law is that you cannot tell anything by listening to someone's voice. The voice you have been listening to probably belongs to a grandmother with varicose veins, piles and an itchy skin condition. Get out into the real world, meet some real girls and develop some real relationships. You'll find it cheaper and far more satisfying.

## ANOTHER AFFAIR

I recently found out that my husband has been having yet another affair. It is the fourth he has had since we married (to my knowledge). He says that he only has these affairs because he is a sex addict and seems to think that I should feel sorry for him. He wants to know if I will stay with him if he goes to a sex addiction clinic. What do you think?

I think this 'I only sleep around because I'm addicted to sex' excuse is brilliant. But I confess that I suspect that it is frequently used as one of the great manipulative tricks of all time. In one sentence it can serve two purposes: excusing the perpetrator's behaviour and at the same time attracting sympathy. In recent years it has become fashionable to excuse just about any bad behaviour by claiming it is a result of an 'addiction' of some kind. Shoplifters claim they only do it because they're addicted to stealing. And joy riders claim they're obeying an irresistible compulsion to steal cars because they are addicted to speed.

There may well be some individuals who really are addicted but on the whole I think much of this is bullshit. In my view most of these individuals share a strong susceptibility to temptation and a high reluctance to take responsibility for their own actions.

I can't help wondering where this bizarre habit of dignifying and licensing every aberrant human activity as an 'addiction' will end. At the rate we're going it won't be long before the government claim that the mess they've got us into isn't their fault; it's all a result of the fact that they are addicted to screwing up.

My sensitive and usually reliable gut tells me that your husband is a con artist. However much you might be tempted to forgive his faithlessness I would strongly suggest that you throw him, his trousers and his glib, excuse laden tongue out into the street. If he had the guts to say, 'Sorry, love, I was a bad lad. I'll clean out the garage and be nice to your relatives for six months,' he would have behaved with some dignity and deserved a little sympathy and respect. But squirming around and attempting to blame his adultery on an addiction suggests to me that he is a slimy, whingeing little toe rag as well as an adulterer. Chuck the snivelling bastard out and buy a goldfish instead.

## BANANA

I eat a banana every day. Is there any risk of my developing potassium poisoning?

No. But see your doctor if you start taking the short cut to work by swinging through the trees in the park.

## PUBIC HAIR

Does pubic hair have a purpose? Why is it curly?

Back in the days when elastic was still uninvented and when zips and buttons were almost unobtainable, primitive people used to have quite a job holding their loin cloths in place. Lots of people got terribly embarrassed if their loin clothes fell off when they ran about. Tennis courts in primitive Wessex were filled with women squealing and attempting to cover themselves with their balls. Because of this widespread sense of embarrassment pubic hair evolved to become curly and to possess a Velcro-like quality—thus making it easy for people to get their loin cloths to stay in position. (I should, perhaps, mention that some Christian fundamentalists argue that pubic hair was given its Velcro like quality by a kindly and thoughtful god).

When the invention of elastic made Velcro-like pubic hair an unnecessary luxury the tight little curls adorning the human pubic mound started to unwind. In another thousand years pubic hair will be straight again.

Where else but in this column could you learn stuff like this?

## NEW BOYFRIEND

When I recently had a chat with my 15-year-old cousin I discovered that she had a new boyfriend. Her parents don't know about him. At first he sounded very nice but it gradually emerged that he is 26 years old, has just come out of prison and is already stealing cars again. My aunt and uncle are very open minded but would, I know, be horrified to discover what their daughter is up to. Should I tell them? My cousin, who is 17 years younger than me, told me in confidence and will be horrified if I break her trust. If I keep her trust and something bad happens I won't be able to live with myself. And if my cousin eventually tells her parents—and mentions that I knew—what will they think of me?

I don't think you have a right to tell your cousin's parents what she told you in confidence. If you do spill the beans then she will never trust you again—and since she is at an impressionable age and she obviously looks up to you the chances are pretty high that she will never trust anyone again.

Besides, if you tell on her then your cousin will have no one in whom she can confide if things start to get difficult.

And you could trigger a real crisis. If your cousin's parents tell her what you've learned in confidence then your cousin may well decide to leave home. You can probably guess where she'd go. I imagine you'd feel pretty bad if that happened.

I'm afraid that by accepting your cousin's confidence you have taken on an enormous responsibility. You must listen to her, talk to her and explain to her the dangers of this relationship. Maybe you could even meet her new boyfriend to find out whether or not he is really as bad as he sounds.

The one bright spot in all this is that your cousin does seem to have had the good sense to tell you what is going on. If she trusts you enough to tell you something this important then there is a chance that she may listen to your judgement.

## BAD RELATIONSHIPS

Since the age of 15 I have had a string of bad relationships. The first man I had beat me up. Then I got involved with a couple who just used me for sex. The last man I had a relationship with stole the locket that my parents had bought me for my 18th birthday. I would love to find a loving man and settle down. But where can I find someone to trust and how will I know that I can trust him?

Not only can I not tell you where to find someone you can trust but I can't even tell you how you will know that you can trust him when you've found him.

Having exposed my own inadequacies in unprecedented fashion let me quickly restore my fully deserved reputation for invincibility and unlimited wisdom by reassuring you that there are subtle ways in which you can reduce the chances of your being hurt quite so badly in the future. Here are three very simple rules.

First, begin any new relationship tentatively and make any new man earn your trust. At the moment that probably seems very obvious. But at the moment you aren't head over heels in love; you're still smarting from the bad experiences you've had in the past. Your heart doesn't jump every time the phone rings or the door bell goes in case it's him. From your personal history I rather suspect that you're the sort of person who gives your trust very easily. Try to be a little more discerning next time a new man enters your life. This doesn't mean that you shouldn't ever let yourself go and trust a man again; it means that you shouldn't let yourself go and trust a man completely just because you've slept with him. Take your time.

Second, never let anyone else persuade you to do something about which you are sincerely and genuinely unhappy. If you don't want to make up a threesome in someone's bed then don't. It's your body, your life and your choice. If you're uncertain about something, say that you want time to think and if, after thinking, you're still uncertain, have the courage to say 'no'.

Third, spend a little time building up your self confidence and self respect. Both have been shattered and both were probably under-developed before—that was probably why you got into so many unhappy relationships and found it so difficult to say 'no'.

## OBSESSED

We have been married for seven years. For the last year my husband has been obsessed with pornographic movies. I can tolerate them now and again but get angry when he wants me to watch them all the time. He just sits there drooling and breathing heavily.

Dirty movies *per se* shouldn't be a threat to any relationship. But if your husband has become addicted to watching other people having (or pretending to have) sex then he undoubtedly needs alerting to his condition.

There are two ways to do this: the official (slow, lengthy, expensive, painful and ineffective) way and the unofficial (fast, cheap, painless and probably effective) way.

The official way is to talk to your husband and convince him that he needs to approach his doctor and ask for professional help. He (ideally your husband but knowing the rate of mix-ups in hospitals possibly your doctor) will then need to visit a psychiatrist for the next 11 years. During that time the psychiatrist will talk to your husband about his childhood, his relationship with his parents and whether or not he was adequately breastfed. The psychiatrist will prescribe powerful and potentially dangerous drugs and as a result your husband will probably become depressed, moody and irritable. Your husband will be shown dirty movies and given small electric shocks every time he shows any interest in what is on the screen.

After several years of this your husband may lose his job and his confidence. At the end of the treatment programme he will probably be a fully qualified dribbling lunatic.

The unofficial approach is for you to go to the nearest charity shop, and buy your husband a dirty old mac. Wrap the mac up in brown paper, hand it to him with a box of paper tissues and a pile of mucky videos and tell him that since he has become obsessed with blue movies he might as well go all the way and become a sad, lonely, dirty old man. Then, when he's settled down in front of the TV, dress yourself up in a slinky, thigh length dress, suspenders, stockings and high heeled shoes and poke your head round the door to tell your husband that you are going into town to have a good time. Do this every night for a week. If at the end of a week he is still slumped in front of the TV watching simulated sex find yourself a toyboy and run off because the treatment has failed and your husband is probably beyond redemption.

If I were a traditional columnist I would feel obliged to recommend that you follow the first of these two alternatives. Since I am not a traditional columnist I feel free to let you choose the treatment which you think might work best.

Of course, you could always try talking to your husband, explaining your feelings and suggesting that maybe you rent a few old fashioned movies in which the participants keep at least some of their clothes on and—you may need to get him to hold on tight to his chair for this bit—actually talk to one another.

## No ERECTION

I am 65 and have taken up with a woman aged 40. We have been to bed together but I cannot get an erection. Could it be because of the pills I take?

Yes. Many prescribed drugs—particularly some of those which are used in the treatment of high blood pressure or depression—can cause impotence.

## UNWANTED FORESKIN

There is nothing wrong with my penis but I am thinking of having a circumcision since a girl I went with told me that she did not like the fact that I had a foreskin. The one thing that worries me is that when I play with myself I move my foreskin up and down but if I am circumcised I won't be able to do this because I won't have a foreskin and so how will I be able to play with myself?

The absence of a foreskin will not prevent you masturbating. Millions of circumcised males could (if they didn't find the prospect too embarrassing) confirm the accuracy of this statement.

But don't have a circumcision just because of one girl's prejudice. Unless you specialise in sexual relationships with jewesses the chances are that the next girl you meet will prefer a foreskin. And when that happens you'll find that it really is a devil of a game getting a surgeon to fix one back on again. Incidentally, a recent survey of 1000 female evangelical Christians showed that 34% preferred circumcised men, 35% preferred uncircumcised men and 31% couldn't remember but didn't think they gave a damn.

........................................................................

## ADMINISTRATORS

Why are you so rude about administrators? We do an important and difficult job.

No, you don't. You're all a total bloody waste of time, space and money. Quick example. A friend of mine who is a dentist abroad recently had a visit from an official who introduced himself as the local inspector of rotating instruments. (I'm not making it up, honest. Not even I could make up crap like this). The inspector of rotating instruments told my dentist friend that one of the instruments in his surgery had to rotate 10,000 times a minute (it might have been 10,000 times a second or an hour—it doesn't matter and who gives a stuff?).

My friend switched the instrument on and held it, busily rotating as dental instruments often do, about an inch away from the official's nose. 'Count 'em!' he shouted with anger born of frustration. 'You tell me how many times it's going round!'

This sort of thing is all a bit of a joke, I know, but there is a serious side to it. You and I are paying for the inspectorate of rotating instruments.

## SIXTEEN

I am 16 years old and need my own place. But the council say they will only help me if I am pregnant. I know two boys but I don't know which one to choose to give me a baby. One is blonde and I would quite like a blonde baby. But the other boy has a part time job and would probably give me some money to help look after the baby.

The price you're thinking of paying for a flat of your own is too high. I know that the council seems to be encouraging you to get pregnant but as a general rule you should never do anything that a council encourages you to do. Local councils are run by the politically inept and the professionally incompetent. You may think that by deliberately having a baby so that you can get a flat you are tricking the system but in the long run you'll be the loser. Having a baby won't make you more independent—even if it does mean that you get your own flat. The flat will probably be infested with cockroaches and have water streaming down the walls and you'll spend the best years of your teenage life wiping dirty orifices, struggling to get a pushchair up and down 5 flights of stairs and trying to remember the last time you had any fun. Don't do it. If you must leave home and you must find somewhere of your own to live there are a hundred and one better ways to do it. Join the army, join a squat, or best of all save every penny you can until you've got enough for the rent on a small flat of your own.

## CUDDLES

My husband and I have been married for three years and we still haven't had any sexual contact. We cuddle each other for a few minutes most nights but that's as far as it ever goes. When we went to visit our family doctor to find out why I hadn't become pregnant, my husband left the surgery in disgust after our doctor tried to explain how babies are made. He refuses to talk about sex because he says it is dirty. He says he won't seek help because there's nothing wrong with things the way they are. He is very religious and says that god does not approve of pleasures of the flesh.

Wait until your husband is out of the house and then pack everything you value in a suitcase or two. Leave home, move away and find a solicitor to annul your unconsummated marriage. Your husband is a boil waiting to burst.

........................................

## Possibly gay

I am 16 years old and I think I might be gay. Last Thursday, after games, I was in the school changing rooms getting dressed after my shower. Just about everyone else had gone when a boy from the year above me came in, stood next to me and stared for a moment or two without saying anything. Suddenly he said he thought I had a very nice looking penis and did I mind if he touched it. I was too shocked and embarrassed to say anything but I suppose he took my silence for permission because he reached out and touched me. My penis became hard almost instantly. He then played with me and after a few moments I came. He then asked if I wanted to do the same for him. Again I didn't say anything so he unfastened his trousers, took my hand and put it on his penis. After he had come he asked me to go round to his house on Saturday. He said his parents would be out and he would show me other things we could do together. I now feel terribly confused. I have never thought of myself as being gay but I know that I will go to his house. What I find particularly confusing is the fact that I still fancy girls quite a lot.

You may be gay. But it is more likely you are just a normal, heterosexual teenager exploring the world of sex and coming up with a few surprises. Many happily married men had isolated sexual contact with members of the same sex when they were teenagers. Most boys who attend boarding school have some sort of homosexual experience.

But do be careful. One of the easiest ways to contract AIDS is to have sex with another man. Adventures that might have been harmless a decade or two ago may now be deadly. Mutual masturbation is fairly safe but always make sure that you both wear a condom.

## VIRGIN?

Can a doctor tell whether or not I am a virgin?

There isn't a straight 'yes' or 'no' answer to this question. If you've just had sex a few times then no, almost certainly not. But if you've had four children then even a pretty incompetent doctor will be able to tell that you know one end of a penis from the other.

## BENT PENIS

My penis bends to one side when it is erect. It never used to do this. It makes intercourse extremely difficult. When I went to see my doctor about it she just sniggered and told me that at my age I shouldn't be worried about that sort of thing. I am 49.

Your doctor deserves to have her diplomas trapped in a mangle. I suggest that you leave her practice before you need treatment for something complicated like a sore throat. I am constantly amazed at how many really awful doctors there are around. Where the hell do these people train? Dachau? Even Mengele would refuse to be in partnership with some of them.

You are almost certainly suffering from a condition known as Peyronie's disease. The bending is caused by a thickening of the tissues down one side of your penis. When you find a proper doctor he will explain to you that the problem sometimes goes away by itself, sometimes needs injections and occasionally needs surgery. This condition is far more common than most textbooks seem to suggest. I get at least half a dozen letters a week from men suffering from this problem.

Hopefully, your condition will soon be mended.

But I'm afraid that your doctor will remain a moist sexual organ long after you've forgotten about your problem.

..................................................................

## GENE THERAPY

Don't you think gene therapy is wonderful? These scientists will save thousands of life by eradicating hereditary diseases.

I am constantly amazed by the naivety of some readers, though I suspect that someone in your family suffers from a hereditary disease and scientists have persuaded you that if they're allowed to continue with their evil experiments they'll be able to offer you a rosy future. If I'm right then I'm afraid that you've been conned. Most scientists aren't messing around with genes because they want to improve the world. They're doing it to get rich and famous. These fungus brained nutters are putting human genes into mice and pigs and vegetables, for god's sake! It's obscene. And it only needs *one* of them to be crooked or incompetent and we'll all be up to our eyebrows in the brown stuff (or whatever colour it is when the geneticists have finished with us). Let the scientists have their way and in a year or two people will be having conversations like this.

First woman: 'Good morning, Mrs Wrigglesworth. How are you today?'

Second woman: 'Oh, not so bad. I'm just off to the doctor's to have my gills cleaned out and my tail clipped.

How's your little boy, the tomato?'

First woman (with a sniff): 'Bad news, I'm afraid. He's had his call up papers. He's being made into soup on Wednesday.'

Genetic experiments are just another unacceptable face of twentieth century science. The scientists must be stopped before it's too late.

••••••••••••••••••••••••••••••••••••••••••••••••••••••••••••••••••

## Odd breasts

My left breast is slightly smaller than my right breast. Is this normal? My doctor says there is nothing wrong.

According to EC report 467CD/25j the average left bosom (female) measures 1.3 standard European handfuls whereas the average right bosom (female) measures 1.4 standard European handfuls. The modest difference is believed to be due to the fact that most men are right handed. (A standard European handful was defined after measuring the digital-palmar capacity of 1,000 Belgian males).

Worry not, unless the difference in size between your breasts is of such significance that you walk with a limp. Women whose breasts are of grossly noticeable differing sizes may need plastic surgery.

••••••••••••••••••••••••••••••••••••••••••••••••••••••••••••••••••

## Telephone caller

A man I used to go out with before I married telephoned me the other day and asked me to meet him for lunch. He said it would just be for a chat and so I went. It was nice to see him but since then he has telephoned me numerous times and asked me to see him again. I've told him that I am happily married but he says he has nude photos of me which he took when we were together and that if I don't agree to see him he'll show them to my husband. I don't know what to do. I can remember the photos and to be honest they were pretty steamy.

Tell your husband everything. And then tell the police and get them to arrest your slimy former lover for blackmail. He'll probably only get three months probation for this offence but if you can also shop him for not paying his tax he'll probably get another 12 years which is considerably less than he deserves.

............................................................

## CONFUSED

I am due to marry my long-standing boyfriend at Christmas but a few months ago I began an affair with a man I've known for several years. Now I'm terribly confused. I can't imagine not having them both in my life. I can't see a way out of the mess I'm in without hurting one of them—as well as myself. The trouble is that I'm attracted to each of them in different ways.

The first thing you must do is cancel—or at the very least postpone—your wedding. You don't have to tell your fiancé why you're cancelling—but you should do it now before the bandwagon becomes unstoppable. If you don't want to tell him the truth just say that you don't feel ready for marriage yet. Tell him that you're frightened and that you need more time to think and prepare yourself for a lifetime commitment. I don't know which (if either) of these two men is right for you but it's pretty clear that you aren't yet ready for marriage.

............................................................

## ODD DREAMS

I often have very odd dreams. Is it true that it is possible to interpret dreams?

According to dirty old Sigmund Freud, if you dream of anything long and thin, long and thick, short and thin, short and thick, pointed, round, wet, warm, cavernous, blue, red, pink, purple, violet, brown, black, soft, hard, slender, broad, empty, slippery, hilly, succulent, large, hot, milky, spicy, tasty, sweaty, smouldering, solid, firm, flexible, damp, dripping or full then you are over-sexed. And, again, according to Freud if you dream of anything else at all then you are severely repressed. Your underlying urges are all sexually orientated but you are sublimating them. Well, more or less. But then, what did Freud know? He was a pervert.

## IN BED

I was in bed with my new boy friend, Jack, when my ex boy friend let himself into my flat and started hunting around for some CDs which he said belonged to him. I'd forgotten he still had a key. Jack, who was clearly very embarrassed, got up and left and I then had a blazing row with my ex boy friend. Jack—with whom I am very much in love—is now refusing to speak to me. How can I persuade him to come back to me?

I'm not surprised that Jack isn't speaking to you. He's probably never thought of sex as a performance art before. I rather suspect that he may be asking himself why you didn't demand your key back when you and your ex-boyfriend broke up. He may also wonder you didn't scream at your ex boyfriend to get out when he came into your flat uninvited. If you want him back why not try the truth? Explain to Jack that you forgot that your ex-boyfriend had got a key and that you were so shocked when he turned up that you couldn't think clearly. Tell him that you've now got the key back (or had the locks changed) and that you've made sure that your ex-boyfriend has now collected all his CDs and socks. Then tell him (Jack) that you love him, that you're sorry for what happened and that you can't live without him. If he won't return your calls or answer his door send him a loving note with some flowers.

## LESBIAN

I have just discovered that a woman I've known for years is a lesbian and lives with another woman. The two of us sometimes go swimming together and I would now like to stop this because I don't like the idea of being in the changing rooms with her. How do you think I should do this? I don't want to hurt her.

Your prejudices are showing. And your conceit and arrogance are staggering. What the hell makes you think that she is likely to fancy you? Do you imagine that the sight of your naked breasts (which she must have seen a zillion times before without losing control) is suddenly going to throw her into a sexual frenzy and stir her into throwing you down on the changing room floor and raping you with her roll on deodorant? Do your sexual feelings so rule your behaviour that if you found yourself in the men's changing rooms you would automatically leap upon the nearest man? What makes you think that lesbians are less sexually selective than heterosexuals? It seems terribly sad to me that you are prepared to discard a long friendship on the basis of your own rather juvenile prejudices and unjustifiable fears.

## SKINNY

However much I eat I never seem to put on any weight. All my friends say I'm lucky but I hate being skinny. Whatever the experts might say I know from bitter experience that men prefer plump women. I don't want to look like a Sumo wrestler but I wouldn't mind looking a bit more like Dolly Parton.

I think you're probably right about men preferring plump women. Most of the surveys which have been done have shown that men find bigger women sexually more attractive while they find very thin women rather intimidating.

'Bony women are OK at a distance but they aren't much fun close up,' said an irretrievably sexist acquaintance of mine. Your problem isn't by any means unique, by the way. Millions of men and women are desperate to put on weight. The Japanese Sumo wrestlers are the world experts at getting fatter so even though you don't want to look like one of them try to follow their eating habits. They eat their largest meals late at night and they make sure that they lie down and rest after every meal. They don't snack because nibbling destroys the appetite and their balanced diet includes a good proportion of rice and pasta. They are, however, careful not to eat a lot of fatty food—since too much fat causes heart disease and cancer. There is no guarantee that you'll put extra weight on in the right places so don't put your order in for a reinforced bra just yet. However, since breasts contain a high proportion of fat there is a very good chance that your bust size will increase if you put on weight.

······················································································

## BLUSHES

I blush a lot and I wish I didn't. What is worse I often blush because I have thought of something sexual; usually something I've never done and don't want to do, but find exciting to think about. The more exciting I find the thought, the more I blush. For example, I have one recurring fantasy in which I dream of being kidnapped by a gang of motorcyclists who take me with them and make me their sex slave. They make me do terrible things and it is something I would hate in real life but in my fantasy I enjoy it enormously and I know I blush bright red when I think about it. By the way, is it unusual for a woman my age (I'm 37) to have sexual fantasies?

No one really knows why people blush but the phenomenon is often a result of guilt or fear or anxiety and is commonly triggered off by sexual thoughts of one sort or another.

To try to stop yourself blushing begin by making a list of all the things you think about that make you blush. Put the most provocative thoughts, the ones which make you blush most, at the top of the list (for example, your scene with the motorcycle gang) and the least provocative thoughts at the bottom of the list. Then, deliberately bring the thought at the bottom of your list into your mind and try to stay as calm and as relaxed as you can. (It is essential that before you try this you learn a good relaxation technique.) If you feel yourself starting to blush banish the fantasy from your mind and just concentrate on relaxing. When you can think about the least provocative fantasy on your list without blushing move up to the next thought on your list. It'll take some time but eventually you should be able to allow each of your fantasies into your mind while staying so relaxed that you do not blush.

I have to warn you that there is one snag: you may find that you enjoy your fantasies less when you can think about them without blushing.

Finally, no, it's not unusual for women of your age (or any age come to that) to have sexual fantasies. The faraway look in the eyes of the prim lady in the tweed suit in front of you in the supermarket queue may be due to something far more exciting than the price of prunes. Remember that there is frequently no correlation at all between what people fantasise about and what they would enjoy in real life. Some of the fantasies enjoyed by vicars' wives would make a stripper blush. Well, perhaps not. But you know what I mean.

..........................................................

## EMBARRASSED VIRGIN

I am getting married in three months time and I am slightly embarrassed that I am still a virgin. Indeed, I think it highly likely that I will still be a virgin on my wedding night. My fiancé is a strict evangelical Christian.
Not only am I not a virgin but I have never even seen an

erect penis. I saw my brother's penis once when he had just come out of the shower but it was, of course, quite limp at the time. I must admit that it did not look very impressive when compared to the stories I have heard from my friends.

I have thought about asking my brother to let me have a peep at his penis in what I suppose could be called the working position but I have not yet plucked up the courage to do this. Do you think I should?

Please stop worrying and please don't bother enlisting your brother's help as an unofficial sexual anatomy tutor. Take some pride from the fact that you will probably be the only girl for a decade to be a virgin on her wedding night. If you want to know what to expect (and what to do when your new husband unlocks his underpants and releases the beast) pop into your local library and borrow a sex manual.

You may also like to take some slight comfort from the fact that even though wedding night virgins are about as rare on the ground as sensitive, intelligent cabinet ministers (the phrase 'intelligent cabinet minister' is, indeed, an excellent example of an oxymoron), ignorance on these matters is far more common than you might think.

A girl I trained with once unwittingly entertained a large lecture theatre full of students by making it fairly clear that she believed that the penis had a bone in it which ensured that it always pointed upwards. She persisted with this view throughout a lengthy and otherwise learned and dry discussion of the male urogenital system and it gradually became clear to us that her past encounters with her several boyfriends had all been inconclusive. Her experiences of the male organ had been limited to visual and digital contact during the tumescent phase and she was, therefore, blissfully unaware of the fearful consequences of ejaculation and the influence of gravity over a wilting organ.

## OLD PEOPLE

My father and mother are both in their seventies and live in a small terraced house where they have lived together since they were married 53 years ago. The house is damp, has no central heating and has a very steep staircase. I am constantly terrified that one of them will fall and I think that they would both be safer and better off living in an old people's home. If they sold their house the money released would be enough to pay for comfortable accommodation for quite a few years. My brother and I have discussed this and feel that we would rather my parents used their money for themselves; neither of us needs any inheritance. How can we get our parents out of their house? They are quite stubborn and will not think about moving.

You could cosh them, wrap them in an old carpet and throw them into your car boot. Or you could hire an arsonist to set fire to their home so that they have no choice.

I realise that your motives are honourable but if your parents are prepared to accept the risk involved in staying in their own home then you should accept the risk too. There are, indeed, sound medical reasons why they should stay where they are. There is now clear evidence showing that when old people are taken out of familiar surroundings they tend to deteriorate quickly, both mentally and physically. If they are moved into an old folks' home your parents are likely to become disorientated and confused. What's more the chances of one of them falling and breaking a bone will be greater too.

I suggest that you stop trying to interfere and allow your parents to stay where they are happy.

How would you like it if a well meaning relative came along and decided that you would be safer in some form of institution?

## TRAIN JOURNEY

I recently went on a long train journey. I had booked a seat and had looked forward to being able to catch up on a few letters and a little reading but the entire journey was spoilt by two extremely ill behaved small children who kept running up and down the aisle shouting and generally making a nuisance of themselves. Their parents did not seem able to control them and although the father shouted at them once or twice the children took no notice of him. What would you have done in my place? I was very tempted to tell the children off myself.

Why on earth didn't you say something? Travelling is tiring enough without having to do it in the company of other people's ill behaved brats.

Next time this happens to you (and there undoubtedly will be a next time because there seem to be regiments of parents who feel that they will stunt their children's development if they attempt to restrict their behaviour in any way) I suggest that you politely but firmly tell the unruly children to behave themselves.

The unruly children will be so shocked by your temerity that they will rush back to their parents and complain. The parents will glare at you, gather up their vast quantity of belongings and leave the carriage in high dudgeon. You will be an instant folk hero among your fellow travellers.

## BRA & PANTIES

Six years ago when my husband was 48 years old he suddenly told me that he wanted to wear a bra and panties. I was surprised but not shocked and because mine were too small I went shopping and bought what he wanted. Since then I've done this regularly for him. It has never bothered me and he is a good lover and husband. Is this common among men?

Yes. Massive numbers of men hurry off to work wearing lacy underwear beneath their dark suits, police uniforms and sports jackets and flannels. Honest. I'm not kidding. Next time you watch a pompous politician or self important celebrity on TV ask yourself whether he could be wearing flimsy, feminine underwear.

........................................................

## VERTIGO

I suffer from vertigo. The newspapers always seem to be full of 'breakthroughs' in the treatment of rare diseases. But my doctor can't help even though he admits that it is quite a common problem.

Medical researchers aren't much interested in common diseases. For reasons which would take a page to explain there is more cash and kudos to be earned by investigating the uncommon and bizarre. However, there are many possible causes of vertigo and there are some treatments available. I suggest that you ask your doctor to fix you up an appointment with an Ear, Nose and Throat specialist.

........................................................

## BROTHERLY LOVE

My brother and I have been living together as husband and wife for 17 years. We are now both in our 50s, are wonderfully happy together and love each other very much. Our sex life is mind blowing. Why does society disapprove so much of our sort of love?

Simply because if close relations married and had children the incidence of inherited physical and mental disease would rocket. Since you seem to have no plans to have children together I wish you both all good fortune.

## SECOND OPINION

My doctor has refused to arrange a second opinion for me even though I am unhappy with the treatment he is giving me. Can he do this?

Technically, yes. But if he is aware of your dissatisfaction and still refuses to arrange a second opinion then he is dangerously arrogant and I strongly suggest that you find yourself another doctor.

## NO MAGIC

I got married fifteen years ago but there was never any magic in our marriage. About a year ago I started to go out with friends once or twice a week, leaving my husband at home watching TV. On one of these nights out I met a man with whom I started a passionate affair. He was married too and although we often talked of running away together it never seemed to be anything more than just a dream. A month or so ago my lover told me that he thought it was time we left our partners and started a proper life together. I asked him if he was sure and he said he was so I went home and told my husband that it was over between us. I then rang my lover to tell him I'd done it. He told me that he couldn't do it and hadn't told his wife. I have now lost everything. My husband is divorcing me and I am living in a tiny room in a run down building in a seedy part of town. Now that we can be seen together my lover doesn't want anything to do with me. I think he is perhaps frightened of what I might do now that I am free. My life with my husband wasn't great but it was comfortable and now I have nothing. Everything is a real struggle. I have difficulty doing my job and I spend my evenings crying. How can I persuade my lover to leave his wife as he promised to do?

I am surprised that you still want to have anything to do with your lover after the way he has treated you. I can imagine that there might be one or two women around who might have stormed into his home, told his wife everything and then made it clear to him that they didn't ever want to see him again.

Do you love him?

That is really the key question.

If you love him then you're going to have to put up with him being an invertebrate.

But if you don't truly Love him (with a capital L) and you want him only because you're lonely and frightened then dig deep into your soul for the strength to live without him for a man this weak can offer you nothing but a future filled with disappointments, despair and sadness.

What do you want to do with your life? Where do you want to live? You have time and freedom. Those are things that most people have too little of; but they can be intoxicating and frightening assets. To conquer them, and to take advantage of them, you must have plans and ambitions. Time and freedom can be powerful and a source of great joy if you control them but they can be enervating and dispiriting if they are not controlled. To take charge of your life, and give yourself hope, you must decide what you want to do and how you want to spend the days, weeks, months and years ahead. Be bold, be brave and be ambitious. The future is yours to do with as you will.

## CONTRACEPTIVE?

My doctor gave me what I think is the contraceptive pill for medical reasons (I have had painful periods). Will this pill stop me getting pregnant if I have sex with my boyfriend?

It probably will if it is the contraceptive pill. But why don't you ask your doctor?

## SURNAMES

I am 19 and have been going out with a lovely man for nine months. I thought that we were very close and had both been honest with each other about our past. Last week a woman started in the office where I work. My boyfriend has an unusual surname and when I learnt that she has the same name as him I casually mentioned the coincidence to her. She told me that it was no coincidence but that my boyfriend is her ex-husband. She said that they had been married for 8 years. I am shattered that he kept such a huge part of his life from me. He says he doesn't see why I am so concerned because his relationship with this woman is over. He says he hasn't lied (which he hasn't) but how can I ever trust him again?

He probably didn't tell you about his previous marriage because he was frightened that it would put you off. He may find his marriage difficult to talk about. Or it may be that he didn't say anything early on in your relationship because he was worried about what your response would be—and then, as the weeks and months went by, he gradually realised that he couldn't tell you because you would want to know why he hadn't told you earlier. I can't believe that he seriously expected to be able to keep this from you for ever.

I don't think you ought to worry too much. Smack his bottom (or refuse to smack his bottom—whichever is going to hurt him most), let him stew for a few more days just to let him know you're peeved, then let him woo you with flowers and then, finally, show him that you forgive him and love him in whichever traditional way you consider most appropriate.

## SELFISH BITCH

I am 24 and have been going out with my boyfriend for

just over a year. I really did think that he was the one for me. He is a very kind and considerate man, though very shy. He has always told me that he loves me and I believe he does. Last week, when we were talking together he dropped a bomb into my life by telling me that when he was a child he was sexually abused by his father. Now I feel tormented. I just cannot tell my family or friends because I know they will be disgusted. And I cannot stand my boyfriend being near me any more. He is totally devastated but I don't think things will ever be the same again for me. Why did he have to tell me?

Two or three times a week I open letters which make me stop, say something extremely rude and get up and walk about the room. Yours was one of these. Having thought about your letter extremely carefully for several days I have decided that you get this month's prize for being the most selfish bitch in the country.

Your boyfriend deserves better than you. I hope that he finds a caring, sensitive, considerate woman who will love him for what he is. How can you give a damn for what your bloody family think? If you loved this boy (and I notice that although you say that he loves you, you don't say that you love him) your heart would go out to him, you wouldn't even think about anyone else, you would understand that he had to dredge his soul to find the courage to tell you of his ordeal.

In all sincerity I just hope that your boyfriend has the strength to tell you to piss off out of his life. You are as deep as a mirror and as faithful as Judas. I bet you're the sort of woman who goes to church every Sunday to show off her latest frock and then looks down her nose at the heathen who don't parade their religion to all and sundry. I hope that you marry a man who has pens in his top pocket and whose pettiness, slyness and insincerity slowly drive you insane. I hope you give birth to two snivelling children who go to university, grow to despise you, and make you realise, in old age, that your entire life has been a waste.

May your orgasms always be elusive and your friends always faithless.

I do hope I've made myself clear.

••••••••••••••••••••••••••••••••••••••••••••••••••••••••••••

## ANTICLIMAX

After spending years making a real effort to delay the moment when I orgasm (in order to satisfy my wife who takes a long time to reach a climax) I now find that I am rarely able to reach an orgasm myself. As you can imagine I find this both frustrating and quite exhausting. Can you please offer me some advice? I am not taking any medicines so it can't be that.

The problem you describe is remarkably common. Men who read this column are, it seems, a remarkably selfless lot. Many have, over the years, consistently disregarded their own pleasures and dedicated their sexual lives to the satisfaction of their partners. After years of holding back in this way the equipment eventually seems to take over and go on strike. There are, however, a number of tricks you can try to trigger an orgasm. Here are a three of the best: contract the muscles in your inner thighs and pelvic area; gently caress your scrotum and testes (this works best if you get your partner to do it); and, finally, stimulate (or get your partner to stimulate) your anal area with your finger tip.

••••••••••••••••••••••••••••••••••••••••••••••••••••••••••••

## SWALLOW

My boyfriend wants me to have oral sex with him but I am afraid of putting his penis in my mouth because when he ejaculates I may end up swallowing his semen. Will I have to have to have my stomach pumped out if he does this?

No. Unless your boyfriend has any infection or the semen goes down the wrong way and you choke (very unlikely) the risks associated with oral sex are very small. Indeed, semen contains a variety of useful nutrients—

including phosphorus, potassium, sodium, calcium, magnesium, zinc, protein, fructose and vitamins C and E—and some people believe that a regular intake of the stuff may improve your health.

· · · · · · · · · · · · · · · · · · · · · · · · · · · · · · · · · · · · · · · · · · · · · · · · · · · · ·

## VEGETARIANS

My husband and I are both vegetarians. When we go to a restaurant that doesn't serve vegetarian food my husband orders salad and chips but I ask for the manager and complain. He says I show him up and tells me not to make a fuss. I think I should say something—otherwise how will they know that people want vegetarian food? What do you think?

I think you're right, though I confess that when I'm tired, hungry and in a hurry I do the same as your husband. To save your husband's embarrassment maybe you could decide what you're going to do before you go in—this should give him time to work up a little self righteous anger. Or give him a minute's notice so that he can sidle off to the loo while you deal with the manager.

· · · · · · · · · · · · · · · · · · · · · · · · · · · · · · · · · · · · · · · · · · · · · · · · · · · · ·

## UNWANTED PROMOTION

I have been offered a promotion at work but I really don't want it. I have seen the way other men of my age ruin their health trying to do jobs in management. I don't have a very demanding job but it suits me fine. I regard my 38 hours of work as 'dead time' but as long as I get paid and can enjoy my family and my hobbies I'm happy. I'm healthy and I don't have much stress in my life. I'd like to keep it that way. My wife is more ambitious and she thinks I should take the promotion, which will mean more money and a bit more status for us both. We've agreed to do whatever you think would be wisest.

If you take on the extra responsibility it is bound to affect your life. No one is going to give you extra money and status without expecting you to work harder and probably for longer hours. You'll have less time and your health will probably suffer. Because you don't really want the extra responsibility you will eventually begin to feel angry and bitter. Your relationship with your wife will suffer and may never recover.

On the other hand if you say 'no' to the extra money and status your wife (who is clearly the ambitious one in the family) may feel frustrated.

I feel that you should turn down the promotion and that if your wife still wants more money and status for the family then she should start looking for a career of her own.

## MY SON

My son is going out with a girl who is a member of a small, very religious group. She has persuaded him not to have anything to do with anyone who isn't in the group—including us. What can we do about it?

Much of the pain and misery in this world can be blamed on religion. Your sad experience is by no means unusual. Many fanatical religious group members regard themselves as superior to everyone else. It's a sort of spiritual class consciousness.

The only advice I can give you is to be patient and persistent. Try to make sure that your son knows that you still love him, care for him and want to be his friend.

## DIRTY SEX

Sex is a dirty and disgusting business. I think it is dreadful the way you accept the fact that people have sex outside marriage.

I spy some slight conflict in your thinking here. If sex is dirty and disgusting why should people save it for (and do it with) the partners they choose to marry? Wouldn't it make more sense if they only did it with people they didn't know very well—and possibly didn't like very much? Just a thought.

.............................................................................

## BIG, PINK NIPPLES

I am 17 and have very large pink nipples and the inner lips of my genitalia protrude. Are either of these things likely to turn a man off?

Not in the slightest. On the contrary, many men would find these physical attributes extremely attractive.

.............................................................................

## LOCKED IN

Is it true that it is possible for a penis to become locked in a girl's vagina? I have heard that our local casualty department recently had to treat a couple who hobbled into the hospital covered only by a blanket and embarrassment.

I fear that the story you heard was apocryphal. In other words someone made it up for a laugh. It is a story with a long pedigree. Back in 1923, in Warsaw, there was a story that a young couple had been stuck together while making love in a public garden. The couple were reported to have been pulled apart only after a doctor gave the girl an anaesthetic. After the story appeared in the Polish newspapers the couple were said to have committed suicide. Theoretically, it is quite possible for vaginal muscles to go into spasm and imprison a penis. However, such spasms last only minutes and relax spontaneously.

## SATISFYING MASTURBATION

I masturbate once a week and it leaves me satisfied and relieved. I have heard that women who masturbate eventually stop having periods and become infertile. Is this true?

I get a lot of letters like this. The answer is 'No'. You will not become infertile, hirsute or short sighted through masturbation.

## TOO MUCH TV?

My little girl watches at least four hours of TV a day. Do you think this is too much? Can it do her any harm?

Yes, it is too much if you want her to grow up into a balanced, intelligent human being. And yes, I really do think it can do harm. If your daughter carries on watching four hours of TV every day then by the time she is 18 she will have watched 26,000 hours of TV. That's nearly twice as much time as she will have spent at school. She will have probably been exposed to around 250,000 commercials and she will have seen 20,000 murders in your living room. Add to all that the fact that kids who watch too much TV tend to get fat and unfit. It is probably not surprising that when a group of 4 to 6-year-olds were asked which they preferred —daddy or television—around half said they preferred television. Frightening, isn't it?

## YOUNG GIRL

I am 48 years old. For four months I have been having an affair with a young girl who works at my office. On several occasions recently I have noticed slight chest pains while making love to her. Do you think these could be a sign of anything serious? I have never had these pains while making love to my wife.

Make an appointment to see your doctor soon and tell him what you have told me. I am afraid that there is a chance that the pains you are suffering from could be an early warning sign of heart trouble. Until you've seen your doctor I strongly suggest that you avoid making love to your mistress. A recent survey of 34 men who had heart attacks and died while making love showed that 29 of them had been making love to mistresses. The anxiety and excitement of an extra marital affair can prove a potent combination. Incidentally, the available research shows that making love after a meal is especially dangerous. If you die in the wrong bed it can cause a lot of trouble for everyone. When I was a practising doctor I once spent a harrowing night trying to get a dead man back into a more appropriate bed.

## COLD TRUTH

Is it true that you can tell where you caught a cold by trying to decide where you were exactly 48 hours earlier?

No. Not really. Cold and flu symptoms begin between 18 and 48 hours after contact with the virus.

## SIT DOWN

My mother always told me that I should sit down for an hour after a meal to give my body a chance to digest the food properly. But my wife says that if you sit down after a meal you're more likely to store the food as fat. Who's right?

I hate taking sides but your wife is more right than your mother. You should be careful not do anything too strenuous or anything that makes you feel nauseous but gentle exercise after eating (such as walking) will not only help the digestive process more than slumping in a chair, it will also help burn up calories. Sitting down after eating is a good way to make sure much of the food you've eaten turns into fat.

## TOE SUCKERS

Is it true that some people get sexual satisfaction out of sucking each other's toes?

Feet are very rich in nerve endings and so they are very responsive to stimulation. Some people claim that they can reach sexual satisfaction by having their toes sucked or fondled. Politicians are particularly fond of toe sucking because they're used to putting their feet in their mouths.

## NO DATES

I am too embarrassed to ask a girl for a date because my penis is so small. Do you think any girl would ever go out with a man with a small penis? Can I have an operation to make it larger? A friend told me that masturbation will make it get bigger. I've tried that twice a day but it doesn't seem to have made any difference.

Would you refuse to go out with a girl simply because she had small breasts? Would you put an end to a relationship simply because you didn't like the size of your partner's vagina? Assuming that you have answered 'no' to both those questions (and if you haven't then you can keep on worrying for all I care) ask yourself why women should be so different. Do you really imagine that women are so obsessed with penis size that the girl of your dreams is going to run out of the bedroom screaming when you produce a chipolata instead of a salami? Stop worrying. If you do happen to find a woman who responds to a view of your equipment in such a bizarre way you've found a one in a million nutter and you're better off without her. I'm sure that you could find a surgeon somewhere in the world who would perform a penis enlarging operation on you. But I wouldn't recommend it. If your penis is big enough for masturbation it's big enough for sex. Finally, I'm afraid I have to tell you that all your hard work in the bathroom has been wasted if your sole aim is has been to achieve a permanent increase in size. The dramatic increase in penis size produced by masturbation is purely temporary.

........................................................................

## RESPONSIBILITY

I work as a clerk in a solicitor's office and have a great deal of responsibility. No one really seems to understand the pressure I am under at work. My wife, who also works but has a far less responsible job, expects me to help her in the home when I get back at night but I just want to sit down and put my feet up in front of the television. I am not a sexist but how can I best explain to her that the stresses of my job mean that I need to relax more than she does?

Have you ever seen M*A*S*H during your long hours resting in front of the TV? Imagine you are a doctor working alone in a casualty department. Your job is to decide whether to treat the man whose leg has been almost completely severed before or after the child with a serious head injury. That's responsibility, that's pressure and that's stress. Stop feeling so damned sorry for yourself, stop dramatising and stop exaggerating the importance of your job. No one is going to die if you file the wrong piece of paper in the wrong drawer. And who, pray, decided that your wife has a less responsible job than you have? Your wife might not have to worry about putting bits of paper in the right drawer but she will have stresses and pressures of her own to cope with. You're not only sexist but you are also patronising and condescending. Stop it. Helping in the kitchen would do you far more good than slumping down and watching rubbish on the box.

........................................................................

## STOCKINGS & SUSPENDERS

My boyfriend says that I should wear stockings because

they are healthier than tights. Is he right or is he just trying to get me to wear stockings (something which I know he likes)?

Stockings are healthier than tights. The largest single factor contributing to the current epidemic of candida (also known as thrush) is the widespread popularity of tights and the demise of stockings and suspenders. Coincidentally, a recent survey showed that three out of four men are turned on sexually if they think a woman is wearing stockings and suspenders. The fourth man probably isn't turned on by anything.

## SUNBEDS

I am 18 years old. My girl friend and I both spend several hours a week on sunbeds. Can this be dangerous?

Unless you are a lesbian I assume that you are male. What a strange, vain fellow you are. I had, I confess, always thought of sunbed use as an exclusively feminine activity. I can understand women (pressurised by society to look glamorous) risking their health on a sunbed. But why would a man be so daft? Lying on a sunbed is as dangerous as spending time in the sun. You risk getting burnt, developing cancer, damaging your eyes and acquiring wrinkles.

## ELECTRIC SHOCKS

I have recently taken a job as a secretary in a large, modern office. I often get small electric shocks when opening one of our metal filing cabinets. Several of my colleagues have noticed a similar problem. Can you tell us how we can avoid this?

The electric shocks are caused by the generation and accumulation of stored energy or static electricity created by the friction of your shoes on the carpet. (I assume that your office is carpeted). These shocks are only felt on discharge and are usually noticeable if a large amount of electricity has been allowed to accumulate. You should be able to get rid of electricity in small, unnoticeable amounts by touching objects more often when you move about. I also suggest that you ask your boss to request the maintenance department to consider increasing the relative humidity in your office since a low humidity seems to make shocks more likely.

## SHOCKING UNDERWEAR

This is a very difficult letter for me to write and I suspect that you might find it difficult to believe, though it is all true. I recently took delivery of a parcel which I opened in error. It contained some very sexy underwear which my wife had clearly ordered from a mail order company though I had never seen her wearing anything like it at home. There were two bras that obviously would not cover any woman's nipples, some brief panties and a suspender belt and stockings. When I confronted my wife she admitted that the clothes were for her and that she had been making extra money by going to bed with men she meets at the restaurant where she works as a waitress. Apparently the restaurant owner knows about it and lets her use a spare room in exchange for half of the money she earns. She keeps what she calls her 'other working clothes' in the room. I was shocked when she told me this but after I had thought about it for a while I became sexually excited by the thought of what she had been doing. My wife has always been very highly sexed and in the past I have been aware of the fact that I have not been able to satisfy her as often as she desired. I would rather that she had sex with strangers rather than entered a more emotional relationship with someone who might take her away from me. Furthermore, my wife insists that without the extra money we could not manage. What do you think I should do?

I thought at first that this letter was a tease. But after checking with the telephone directories for your area I'm convinced that it isn't. People writing spoof letters don't usually give their real names and addresses and they don't use words like 'furthermore'. I was suspicious because some men do get excited by the idea of their wives making love to strangers, though this is usually nothing more than a fantasy. However, since in your case the fantasy seems to have come true you have to face the fact that you both run a risk of contracting a sexually transmitted disease and being arrested. Your wife could minimise (though not eradicate) the first of these risks by insisting that her clients wear a condom but the only way to minimise the second risk is to ensure that your wife's activities do not become too widely known. From what you have said I think you may well be right about your wife's sexual behaviour being less of a risk to your marriage than an ordinary affair—as long as you can truly come to terms with it. My only practical advice is that you should perhaps have a word with the restaurant owner. He seems to me to be charging your wife rather a high percentage of her earnings.

## EXTRA PENIS

Is it possible for a man to have an extra penis? My girl-friend says it is. I say it's impossible. Who's right? Whoever wins the bet has to pay a sexual forfeit so please let us know your answer as soon as possible. And would you choose the forfeit?

Your girlfriend wins. One in every 5,000,000 men has an extra penis. These men can (in theory at least) make love to their wives and commit adultery at the same time. When men have an extra penis both organs are usually capable of a full erection so the owner is unlikely to know whether he's coming or going. A man could, of course, have one penis circumcised and the other left with a complete foreskin. It would, I suppose, be perfectly possible to use the two organs concurrently or consecutively. Your forfeit is simply to know that this is true and that you are not one of the chosen few.

••••••••••••••••••••••••••••••••••••••••••••••••••••••••••••••••••••••••

## RECOVERY TWADDLE

Is it true that a woman's chances of making a good recovery from breast surgery for cancer depend upon the time of the month that she has the operation? My doctor says he hasn't heard of this and thinks it is probably 'twaddle' (his word).

Published evidence suggests that far more pre-menopausal women survive breast surgery if they have an operation which is done during the second half of their menstrual cycle than if they have an operation in the first two weeks of their cycle. This difference can probably be explained by the change in hormone levels which occurs during a period. If researchers put more effort into studies of this sort and wasted less time and money on pointless research such as animal experiments far more lives would be saved. The link between breast cancer and the menstrual cycle was first observed in 1836 (yes, 1836—over 150 years ago) so I really don't understand why more research hasn't been done to find out the precise link between hormone levels and cancer. I honestly don't think anyone knows *for certain* whether or not the time of your operation will really affect your survival chances. But if I was a woman having breast surgery for cancer I would want to have the operation done in the second half of my menstrual cycle.

••••••••••••••••••••••••••••••••••••••••••••••••••••••••••••••••••••••••

## ASPIRING ACTRESS

I want to be an actress but everyone says I stand no chance. They say that most actresses are permanently out of work and that the chances of my succeeding are ridiculously slim. My family and my boyfriend want me to apply for a job in our local bank. But I've been offered a place in a drama school. What do you think I should do?

It all depends on how much you really want to be an actress and whether you are prepared to take a chance with your life. What's the worst that can happen if you try and fail? You might, I suppose, have to put up with people telling you that they told you so. But at least you'll have tried. If you don't try, if you don't take a chance, then you won't fail, of course. But in twenty, thirty or forty years time you may well look back on your life and regret the fact that you never tried to fulfil your ambition. There are fewer things that are sadder than hearing someone say: 'I wish I'd had the courage to try...' when it's far too late for them to give their ambition a chance. If you don't try then you'll never know what would have happened.

If you do decide to take a chance then you must have faith in yourself. If you set out on an acting career convinced that you will fail then you'll almost certainly fail. But if you set out believing that you can succeed—well, at least you'll be in there with a real chance.

Believing that you can do something is the hardest thing in the world—but one of the most important things in the world if you really want to succeed at something.

For years thousands of athletes tried to beat the four minute barrier for the mile but everyone thought it was an impossible target and so no one managed it. And then an athlete called Roger Bannister succeeded. The year after Bannister had proved that the impossible was possible thirty other runners completed the mile in under four minutes. And the year after that three hundred runners broke the four minute barrier. Nothing had changed. A mile was still as long as ever. And four minutes was still 240 seconds. But, suddenly the impossible had become possible because Roger Bannister had the faith to take on the impossible.

## SHAVER

I am a 37-year-old woman. I have excessive body hair around my genital area and thighs. Is there any treatment I can try to get rid of it? I have to shave before I can wear a bikini. My doctor has given me creams to try and I have even visited a specialist at the hospital but they said I just have a lot of pubic hair and that they couldn't help. I really do envy those models with their silky smooth legs. I would love to be like them.

The only permanent way to remove unwanted body hair is by electrolysis. I'm afraid that if you have a large area of hair to remove this remedy is likely to be expensive. A tiny needle is inserted into the hair follicle and a small electric current used to destroy the root of the hair. The hair can be pulled out and there will be no more growth. If you choose this method make sure that you visit a properly trained specialist.

Don't be too envious of glamorous looking models, by the way. Most of the ones I've met have been constantly worried about their looks. Even the most beautiful and apparently faultless beauties seem to manage to find something to feel concerned about. If hairy thighs and a superabundant pubic bush are your only worries you aren't doing too badly. Anyway, in Spain or Italy where women with lots of body hair are considered a turn on, you'd be a pin up.

## ONE-OFF THING

I came home early two weeks ago and found my boy friend in bed with my mother. They both insist that it was just a one-off thing and that we should all carry on as if nothing had happened. But I find this difficult. My boy friend and I live at home with my mother and every time I go out and leave them together I worry about what is happening. What do you think I should do?

First, decide whether or not you want your relationship with your boyfriend to continue.

Do you love him?

You're stuck with your mother but your boyfriend is expendable.

If you decide you don't want the relationship to continue then either he or you will have to move out. If he won't move out then you will at least know the truth about the relationship between the two of them.

If you love him—and he says he loves you—then you should both look for somewhere else to live. Find somewhere of your own as far away from your mother as possible. Ignore his inevitable protests about it not being so convenient or being more expensive. Find somewhere of your own—even if it's a cardboard box.

········································································

## PIERCED NIPPLES

My girl friend has pierced her nipples with a hot needle so that she can wear ear rings through them. Now she wants to pierce my scrotum. She says it is perfectly safe. Is she right?

No. She's talking absolute balls.

········································································

## LEATHER SKIRT

Seventeen years ago, when I met my husband for our first date, I was wearing a short, black leather skirt and a pair of long black leather boots. They were, I think, rather fashionable at the time and they were certainly the smartest clothes I had. On our way home we made love in a newsagent's shop doorway. I kept my leather skirt, stockings and knickers on and although it was a little uncomfortable it was certainly erotic and very exciting. Since then we have acquired quite a wardrobe of black leather (I even have some black leather underwear) and my husband and I both get turned on when I wear it. My husband even has some black leather clothing of his own and he wears that sometimes too. Do you think there is anything unusual or perverted about what we do? We often wear our leather clothing when we make love.

No. Lots of people get turned on by wearing (or seeing or feeling their partner wearing) particular types of clothing. Leather, rubber and nylon all have their aficionados. There is probably someone somewhere who can be driven wild by the texture of Harris Tweed. Wearing leather only becomes a problem if either you or your husband cannot get sexually aroused, or make love, unless one or both of you is or are wearing something made of black leather. However, do beware about making love in newsagents' shop doorways. I notice from your letter that you live in an area where there is bound to be a local by-law against it.

## SEPARATE ROOMS

My daughter is 25 years old and although she isn't married she lives with a man she works with. He has been married before. When they come to stay I refuse to let them sleep together and make them have separate rooms. My husband supports my point of view but my daughter says I'm being silly because I know that she sleeps with this person the rest of the time. But I don't like the idea of them doing it in my house. Do you think I'm being unreasonable?

No. It's your house. And if you and your husband don't want to encourage any hanky panky then you're quite entitled to keep your daughter and her boyfriend apart. Indeed, you may be doing them a favour. They may find tip toeing along the landing rather exciting.

## FAMILIAR SMELL

After having sex with my boyfriend I notice a smell that seems familiar but which I can't quite place. Can you help me?

Semen smells like horse-chestnut blossom, as you will discover if you stand underneath a horse-chestnut tree at the right time of the year. It is surprising how many bathroom related products are now manufactured with the smell of horse-chestnut blossom.

## DROOPY BUST

My bust is rather droopy. I have seen several creams advertised which are said to help improve the tone and shape of sagging breasts. Do you recommend these creams?

No. Nor do I believe that these creams will banish rust, unblock drains or make tired upholstery look like new.

## NURSE'S OUTFIT

Two years ago my husband, Geoff, bought me a skimpy nurse's outfit for our anniversary. I put it on to please him and it certainly seemed to get him very excited. Since then he has bought me quite a variety of sexy clothes including a French maid's costume and several bras which have holes for my nipples to poke through. I don't mind wearing these clothes for him but he now wants me to serve dinner in my French maid's costume when two business contacts of his come to our home next week. The skirt is so short that it barely covers my bottom and the top is so low cut that if I bend forward my breasts (which are quite large) fall out. I'm worried that the visitors might get the wrong idea but Geoff says it'll help break the ice and might help him get an important order. When I objected he pointed out that I have worn more revealing clothes on the beach. I couldn't think of an answer to that because he was, of course, absolutely right. What do you think?

I don't think Geoff is as interested in getting an important order as he is in displaying your assets to his guests. Say 'No' unless you want to be served up as the *spécialité de la maison*. Make it clear that while you don't mind dressing in revealing clothes for him, you don't want strangers feasting on your nibbly bits when they should be nibbling on your feasty bits. There is a lot of difference between wearing a revealing bikini on the beach and wearing a revealing skimpy costume in front of a couple of guests in your own home.

## SERVANT

My married lover likes to pretend that he is my servant when he is with me. Although he has a very important job as a solicitor he gets turned on when I make him do the housework around my flat. He does the washing, the ironing and the cleaning dressed only in a very flimsy pink pinafore which just about covers his private parts. When he has finished I have to inspect his work and punish him if it isn't perfect. Needless to say there is always something I can find fault with and I then shout at him and spank his bare bottom with a cane (I used to use my hand but he likes me to hit him quite hard and I found that it was hurting me as much as him). He always has a huge erection when I've finished spanking him and we then make love. How unusual is this and is it anything to worry about? Incidentally, since you seem to have a good sense of humour you may be amused to know that there are one or two unusual advantages to this relationship. I have the cleanest flat of anyone I know but my hands look so nice that no one believes I don't have a cleaning lady.

This sort of behaviour is far commoner than you might imagine, though most of the men who enjoy ritualistic humiliation go to prostitutes who specialise in this sort of thing. One prostitute I know has so many 'slaves' who like doing her washing that she can't dirty her clothes fast enough. All her friends give her their underwear and get it back washed and ironed free of charge. Does your lover like being humiliated while he does gardening, by the way? Maybe you could send him round to my place in the summer.

## INSTINCTS

Do you believe in instincts?

A year ago my husband met a man who wanted him to go into partnership with him. I didn't like the man and advised my husband to have nothing to do with him. I couldn't explain why but just said it was my 'instincts'.

My husband said I was being irrational, and on the basis of recommendations from his accountant and his bank manager, went into the business with the man.

As a result of that partnership my husband lost most of our money. We had to sell our car and move to a smaller house.

Three months ago I refused to get onto an aeroplane because I had a bad feeling about it. At the time my husband was very cross with me because it meant that a long awaited and much needed holiday had to be cancelled and we lost quite a lot of money (none of which we could afford to lose). When he found out afterwards that the plane had developed an engine fault over Spain and had very nearly crashed he was a bit more understanding.

I think instincts are very powerful and that most of us underuse them.

Despite these two experiences my husband is still sceptical and I know I would find it difficult to persuade him to trust my instincts (or his own) in the future.

I think you are absolutely right—instincts are important and should be trusted.

Many apparently sensible and intelligent people have great difficulty in making relatively simple decisions such as which food to order in a restaurant or what to wear when going out for the evening. Time and time again you will see people creating stresses and anxieties for themselves because they don't trust their initial instincts. Ironically, they frequently end up by ordering or putting on whatever it was that they had almost chosen by instinct right at the beginning.

Those individuals could benefit a lot if they learned to make up their minds to trust their instincts. They would make decisions more speedily. There would be fewer regrets and much less unnecessary anxiety.

The unconscious mind can often prove helpful when there are bigger problems to be overcome.

If you can't think of an answer to a difficult problem, try relaxing or doing something completely different and then coming back to your problem later. Allow your subconscious mind to go to work and when you return to the problem you'll probably find a solution waiting for you.

Learn to listen to your inner self and you will find a peace and a calm that you might have never thought possible.

You are clearly well connected to your instincts. I think you're right to say and do what your instincts tell you is right.

·············································································

## MORE EXPERIENCED

When I was eighteen and still a virgin I met a man who was much older than me and, naturally, far more experienced sexually.

The very first time we slept together he wanted me to have anal sex and because I was very innocent and I thought that this was normal I said 'yes'.

After about three months (during which time we had anal sex just about every night) I left him after he had tried to persuade me to do something else which I will not describe. Ever since then, however, I have suffered from a variety of bowel problems.

The two main symptoms are constipation and wind though occasionally I get a colicky pain in my lower abdomen as well. I have seen four doctors so far and none of them has been able to find anything wrong. They all just tell me to go away and stop worrying, but I'd like your advice.

Do you think it is possible that my back passage was permanently damaged in some way by the anal sex? It surely isn't normal to have sexual relations that way.

The man concerned was very well endowed and subsequent experience has taught me that his sexual organ was much larger than the average.

Even when we had sex the normal way I didn't really enjoy it because it was so painful; when we had anal sex the pain used to make me cry.

I get a lot of letters about anal sex—mostly from women. Some are from women who worry about whether it is normal or not and some from women who are concerned that having had anal sex may have caused them some permanent injury. One in ten heterosexuals regularly practise anal sex and more than fifty per cent of heterosexuals have tried it—so it certainly isn't abnormal.

Because regular anal sex can lead to stretching of the normally tight anal sphincter it may eventually lead to incontinence.

There are two other important ways in which anal sex can cause physical damage.

First, if anal and vaginal intercourse are mixed then there is a risk that bacteria from the intestinal tract may be introduced into the vagina. To minimise the risk vaginal sex should precede anal sex and two condoms (worn consecutively) should be worn instead of one.

Second, the risk of transmitting the AIDS virus from one partner to another is very high during anal sex, though the use of a strong condom will reduce the risk of AIDS being transmitted.

However, even an unusually large penis is unlikely to do any permanent physical damage to the bowel itself and I rather suspect that your symptoms may be a result not of your unhappy physical sexual experiences but of the mental consequences. You are clearly still extremely worried about what happened to you when you were a teenager and it could well be that you now have a condition created by stress and anxiety rather than by the anal sex itself. You could, for example, be suffering from the irritable bowel syndrome. I suggest that you ask your doctor to refer you to a gastro-enterologist.

## SHOW BUSINESS

When I met my boyfriend I was working in a pub. The manager used to book various acts. That night we had a hen party with a male stripper. I was talking to a really nice man sitting at the bar. He asked me to go for a drink the next day and I said I would. I couldn't keep talking to him because we were busy and I didn't see him again until the stripper came on. It was him. I didn't turn up the following night but he kept coming back to the pub and finally he persuaded me to go for one drink. We had such a good time that I agreed to see him again. We are now living together. I have accepted his job (he is also a kisso-gram) but now he has told me that a business man he knows has offered him a large amount of money to put on a sex show at a private party. There is no question of group sex—just the show. My boyfriend has asked me to do it with him. The money would enable us to put a deposit on a house. I think they want to video us. I am scared to do it. However, if I don't he will go with someone else. Do you think it will be wrong? After all we will only be making love to each other. Please advise me.

Do you want to do it? Do you think you can do it? Are you happy to make love to your boyfriend with a group of other people watching? And are you happy to be filmed making love—knowing that the video could well end up on the stag night circuit? The video in which you star could make someone a lot of money but could have a big impact on your life in the future. What if you and your boyfriend split up and you want to marry someone who doesn't know about this episode? The existence of a video could haunt you.

If you don't want to have sex in public then say 'no'. If you're prepared to do the sex but don't want to be filmed make it clear what you will and won't do.

And if you don't want to do it and don't want your boyfriend to have sex with another woman tell him. But before you put your foot down decide how far you're prepared to go. If he ignores you are you going to leave him? Make up your mind and tell him.

If you say 'yes' then you should lay down the ground rules with your boyfriend. What are you (and your boyfriend) going to do if one of the spectators wants to make love to you? What are you (and your boyfriend) going to do if one of the spectators tries to touch your naked body? You must think about these things beforehand and know exactly what you are both going to do—and you must insist that he makes the rules clear to the party organiser beforehand.

And are you going to do it again? I know you're doing it this time to get the deposit for your house but there will always be a reason. Next time it will be to pay for curtains and carpets. Then there will be furniture. And a fridge. And a car. And a holiday in the Seychelles. And where are you going to draw the line? What if one night a stranger offers you a vast sum to masturbate him to orgasm? What if two strangers offer your boyfriend an even bigger sum of money if you'll make love to them both? What would your boyfriend say? How far are you prepared to go?

## RESENTFUL

When I first got married I really looked forward to having children. But I now have two children (one aged 12 and the other aged 14) and although I love them dearly I'm afraid that there are times when I get fed up and resentful about the way they run my life. Sometimes it seems that every waking hour of my life is spent either looking after them or making money to buy them 'essential' clothes, trips or computer software. They never seem to be grateful for anything that is done for them and they sometimes treat my wife and I as though we are servants.

This is a column about human problems and so I don't usually try to provide advice for or about teenagers, social workers, refugees from the planet Zog, politicians or others who cannot, by any stretch of the imagination, be regarded as members of the same race as the rest of us. However, the anguish shone out from your letter and so I feel inspired to offer a few thoughts which might be of help.

First, you should be aware that your feelings are by no means unique. The streets and suburbs are populated by individuals who started out their lives full of hope, ambition and pride but who have, through parenthood, been turned into dull and weary 'grown ups'; suffocated by awesome responsibility and spiritually dead from the hair downwards. Males who once concerned themselves with such essentials as the price of real ale and remembering to keep their wallets stocked with condoms, and whose main weekly responsibility was getting up early enough on a Sunday to get to the football pitch before the game started, suddenly start worrying about the price of chocolate covered Puff Puffs, and spend their Sunday mornings fitting safety gates at the top of the stairs and rear seat belts in the grey four door sedan which they got when they sold the red sports car. Overnight, girls who only ever worried about visible panty lines and hairspray suddenly become obsessed with finding the safest push chair and the best buy alphabet spaghetti.

You say that you looked forward to having children before you had them and I'm sure you are right. All newly weds are encouraged to believe that they are obliged to 'start a family' as soon as they can. This, it is widely understood, is the price that has to be paid for having access to unlimited sexual opportunities. If you think back you will, I suspect, recall that you were heartily encouraged in this aspiration by those whose views you regarded as valuable—and, in particular, by your parents and your partner's parents. This is significant and I will return to this in a moment.

Only when it is too late to push the damned things back in do you discover that newborn babies are cute and marginally sufferable only up until the age of about twelve months. After that the rapidly growing beasts gradually become increasingly boring, tiresome and demanding. Only the rich, who can afford to hire a nanny and see their children for no more than half an hour in the evenings, stand any chance of surviving. Faced with unending demands from the cuckoo in their nest (for the first few years the demands are for food but as time goes by the demands become more sophisticated and expensive) the average pair of parents quickly lose spirit and self respect.

Most parents lose any vestiges of hope when their ungrateful children finally turn into whining teenagers. At this point life seems hopeless. Teenagers automatically despise their parents, compete with their friends to see who can run up the biggest telephone bill and treat their parents with the greatest amount of contempt and disdain.

I can, however, offer you a chance for the sweetest revenge. Hold this thought close to you during the coming months and years. It will sustain you in your darkest moments.

When your children finally metamorphose into young adults you can get your own back by encouraging them to marry *and to have children of their own!*

What joy this thought will bring you. The thought of your grotesque and loathsome offspring, who have taken over your life, cursed with children of their own should bring a smile to your lips on the darkest of days. And now, at last, you will realise why your own parents were so keen for you to start a family.

## ORGANISED RELIGION

What are your views on organised religion? My boyfriend is a very religious person. I am not. I can accept his need to worship his god but he won't accept that I don't feel the same way. Do you think I should give in to keep him happy or do you think I would eventually feel so hypocritical that I grew resentful?

Your boyfriend's behaviour puzzles me. What possible reason can there be for forcing you to pretend to worship his god? If his god is as wise as he obviously thinks he is then he will quickly see through your masquerade. I can't help feeling that your boyfriend is trying to influence you for very earthly reasons. Maybe he wants to show you off to the choir. Maybe his parents will give him a hard time if you don't turn up on parade in the family pew.

I have to confess that I find it difficult to see any point in organised religion. If you do what is right and your god approves then you don't need the blessing of a man in fancy dress and you don't need to go down on your knees in a florid building to tell your god how decent you are. He'll know. I can't believe that any genuinely powerful and compassionate god will be influenced by hymn singing or plaster of paris models of the three wise men. On the other hand if he thinks that your behaviour stinks then the blessing of the church still won't persuade your god to give you a season ticket to heaven.

## BABYSITTER

I am a 15-year-old and I babysit quite often for a couple who live nearby. The last time I was there I was asleep in the spare bedroom when the wife came in and sat on the bed. She was naked and she started touching me. I was terrified and got out of bed, grabbed my clothes and went and hid in the toilet until I heard her go back to her own bedroom. I got dressed and ran out of the house and sat outside my own house until 6.30 when my Dad came down and let me in. Now I feel ill and disgusted whenever I think about it. I am also really angry but ashamed as well. I can't tell my parents because this woman is the wife of my dad's boss. I was going to keep quiet because I was so embarrassed but she has given my mum a list of dates for me to babysit. Please help: I feel scared.

Tell your parents what happened. They and you can then decide whether to make a fuss or not. But at least you won't have to worry about going back there if your parents know the truth.

## NO CONFIDENCE

I have recently been thinking about going to a prostitute. I have been celibate for 17 years. I am a normal red blood male but although I love women (I am not gay) I have no confidence with them. Do you think a visit to a prostitute might help give me more confidence?

I doubt it. It'll probably give you a momentary thrill. And if you don't use a condom it might well give you a nasty rash, an unpleasant discharge and a regular chair at the local sexually transmitted diseases clinic. But unless your fear of women is inspired by an unsuccessful sexual experience, and you simply need to build up your confidence by going to bed with a woman who will make you feel like a stud because that is what she is paid for, I don't think a bout with a hooker will help you much.

There is nothing at all wrong with patronising a prostitute. But I think you are mistaken if you imagine that a commercial sexual adventure will give you more confidence when dealing with women who don't want paying before they'll go to bed with you.

I suspect that your reluctance to try to initiate a more normal relationship with a woman may be inspired by your fear that you may be rejected.

If I'm right, then you are suffering from two misapprehensions.

First, you're wrong to assume (as so many men do) that women are all waiting to put men down and get a kick out of making men feel small. Some women probably do. But, believe it or not, most women are just as nervous and apprehensive about relationships as you are. If you ask a woman to go out with you and she says 'no' she really isn't likely to rush off giggling to tell all her friends about how she squashed you. (If she does, you're lucky she said 'no'.)

Second, does it really matter if you are rejected? If you ask a woman to go out with you and she says 'no' you haven't lost anything. You haven't made any progress but things aren't any worse than they were before you asked.

Just remember: men who seem to be successful with women get rejected a lot. But the nine 'no's' don't matter as much as the first 'yes'.

........................................................

## PHOTOGRAPH COLLECTION

My boyfriend keeps a collection of photographs of his old girlfriends. In many of the photos the girls are partly or completely naked. I've asked him to destroy the pictures but he won't. I've let him take photos of me in the nude and I have this awful feeling that one day I'll be just another page in his scrapbook.

I can understand you not wanting to be reminded of the fact that you aren't your boyfriend's first lover. But destroying the evidence won't alter the fact that he wasn't a virgin when he met you.

On the other hand it is tactless and boorish of him not to keep his little black album hidden. If he wants to retain the evidence of his past successes then ask him to at least hide the collection somewhere private so that you can forget about its existence.

And if he insists on keeping his personal dirty picture file you should perhaps keep possession of the photos he's taken of you. You can explain that you don't want to risk becoming part of his two dimensional harem.

................................................................

## No FANTASY

Why do people find it necessary to fantasise about sex? Three years ago I met a wonderful man. Since I did not approve of making love outside wedlock we did not go to bed together. Five months ago I agreed to the inevitable. My man is considerate and sensuous and we never fail to climax together. Sex has really enriched my life. What could fantasy add?

I would like to congratulate you. If you and your boyfriend always climax together then you are either a rare couple or else you haven't done it very often yet. Even the most skilled lovers usually admit to a few misses. However, maybe your sex life is going to be a never emptying bowl of cherries. Maybe God has decided to reward your 31 months of continence by endowing you both with superhuman sexual skills. Having said all that may I humbly suggest that you look at your letter again in six months time. I suspect that you may find yourself blushing at your innocence and smugness.

## A GOOD SIZE

When I have sex with my boyfriend he puts my legs on my shoulders. It really hurts me because he has a good size on him.

Then tell him not to do it. And if he tries to insist grab his balls and squeeze until he sees stars and sense.

## CONDOMS

Would you please put something in your column about the importance of using condoms? I have three teenage sons and none of them use condoms. They say that all the girls they go with are on the pill so they don't need to worry. I don't mind them having fun but how can I persuade them to be careful?

Aren't teenagers stupid? Still, I have it on good authority that all lawyers, bureaucrats and politicians are former teenagers so what do you expect?

Teenagers automatically assume that their parents know nothing so your sons probably assume that wearing a condom is as essential as wearing a clean vest or carrying a hanky.

The contraceptive pill reduced the chances of a single sexual episode resulting in a constantly growing reminder of those few moments of joy.

But babies aren't the only unwanted consequences of sex.

At least 25 different diseases can be transmitted through groin contact sports. One or two of those diseases can be fatal. Nearly all of them can be painful.

Your sons are lucky to have such a broadminded mother and stupid not to listen to her. Buy them a three pack each and don't let them out until they promise to use them.

(Of course, if you've got the guts to try it you could always order them *not* to use condoms. Being bloody minded teenagers, they'll automatically do the opposite.)

## ORGAN SALE

My business collapsed recently leaving me with substantial debts. The bank is threatening to repossess my house. I recently heard about a man who sold one of his kidneys for a large amount of money. Maybe this would be the answer to my problems. How do I go about it? What will I get for a kidney? Are there any other organs I can sell?

I don't know of any reputable surgeon who would remove any of your organs for money. I suggest that you hang onto everything you've got. God gave you two kidneys for a reason. Selling organs so that you can keep going is like selling bits out of your car engine so that you can pay for a tankful of petrol.

## HUNT FOLLOWER

I am 25 and I work in a large office. Even though I now live in a town I still ride regularly with a local hunt. Some of the people I work with don't understand why hunting is necessary to keep foxes and stags under control. Recently, they have started to make my life miserable. A few even refuse to speak to me. I have tried explaining to them that hunting is more than just a sport but they don't seem to understand. I would appreciate your advice.

Stop hunting. It is a barbaric and inhuman activity patronised and supported by lying psychopathic lunatics. I am not surprised that your colleagues refuse to have anything to do with you. Why don't you take up bungee rope jumping instead? Try it with a 100 ft rope and a 60 ft jump.

## HUNT PROTEST

Your recent reply to a letter from a hunt supporter was quite outrageous. If you repeat your libellous comments about people who hunt we will take action against you.

In my view hunters are cowardly, parentally challenged, intellectually deprived, sadistic, bloodthirsty psychopaths and hunt supporters are evil, odious little vandals with the presence and personality of snailshit. May your balls rot and drop off, may your TV set receive only black and white pictures and may your car never start. You are a pathetic, whingeing, snivelling, cryptorchid dickhead with the brains of a TV game show host and the wisdom of a highway bollard. How's that?

## PIN UPS

I was sent a pin up calendar containing 12 pictures of attractive young women wearing very little. I left the calendar on the desk in my private office when I went for lunch. When I returned I found a note telling me to report to my boss. I was told that a complaint of sexual harassment had been made against me by another employee who had seen the calendar. My boss, who won't tell me who made the complaint, has given me an official warning. My job and future career are now in jeopardy.

I have several filing cabinets packed with extremely boring research papers and I slip pin up pictures of naked women amidst the files at random. These pictures are carefully torn from politically incorrect magazines and newspapers which usually come into my possession because I buy them. I do this so that when I'm hunting through a filing cabinet drawer and looking for a series of papers on hypofibrinogenaemia or otorhinolaryngology my eyes will occasionally alight on a picture of a beautiful woman with no clothes on. Looking at a picture of a naked woman may not be particularly enlightening, and the very thought of it may offend some prurient and humourless self appointed guardians of public morality, but it wakes me up, cheers me up and helps me to keep on concentrating—and it does no one any harm—so screw them. I have no doubt, however, that if I worked in your office (or, indeed, most of the offices in existence) the sex gestapo would have long ago marched me out into the car park and shredded my credentials.

The odious and spine chillingly unemotional fascists who disapprove of and violently condemn innocent behaviour, harmless fun and unintended discourtesies whenever they feel that their theoretical boundaries of sensitivity have been threatened are as much of a threat to freedom as any jack booted, goose stepping Nazi ever was or could be.

An army of pseudo intellectual vigilantes, armed with suspicion and wagging fingers, now patrols every aspect of twentieth century life. In the world in which these mind control fascists would have us live jokes and lingerie would be outlawed and our language would be bowdlerised and savaged.

I don't approve of behaviour which is boorish, offensive and hurtful. But you did nothing wrong. Make a stand. Demand that the  official warning you've been given be withdrawn.

......................................................................

## FIRED

I was fired five weeks ago. I have become very miserable and I am having difficulty in picking myself up. I would appreciate it if you could offer me some comfort and advice.

I have lost count of the number of times I've been sacked. I usually get sacked because I've annoyed some important establishment or industrial pressure group. Once I was sacked by a local newspaper editor who carried a syndicated column of mine and who told me that I was being sacked simply and solely because I made people think. Encouraging the readers to think was not something that the editor or his advertisers felt was a necessary part of a newspaper's role.

The fact that you have been fired doesn't mean that you aren't of any value or weren't any good at what you were doing. It may mean that you were too good for the job you were doing or too imaginative, daring or innovative for the place where you were working. You may have been fired solely because of someone else's incompetence or lack of imagination. You may have shown too much initiative or alarmed other workers with your intelligence and perspicacity.

People who regularly do the firing in large companies are a special breed. They aren't usually blessed with many brains (it would be a waste to hire anyone wise to wield the hatchet) and they tend to be humourless and borderline psychotic. Because they aren't too bright they tend to acquire favourite little phrases. One dull hatchet man always tells the people he fires that the firm is giving them an opportunity to explore their talents elsewhere. He uses this phrase because he thinks people will be half way down the corridor before they realise that they've been canned.

You should regard being fired not as an end but as a beginning; it *is* an opportunity to find out what you can really do.

## BREASTS

Why are men so interested in women's breasts?

Males are fascinated with breasts from birth. For the first six months of life the interest is inspired by hunger. Interest then wanes for ten or twelve years. When it returns it is inspired by lust.

## SHOCKED WIDOW

I am a 54-year-old lady who was widowed 2 years ago. I met my late husband when I was 21 and until recently he was the only sexual partner I had ever had.

Six months ago I met a man (a widower) who is 2 years

younger than I am. We got on very well and two months ago we got married and went away on honeymoon. We did not go to bed together until our wedding night.

I had the shock of my life when I saw my new husband in the shower.

I had always assumed that my first husband had an average sized penis (he was the only man I had ever seen naked) but limp or erect his penis was only half the size of my new husband's. When we tried to make love it was a complete failure. The pain was so great that my husband simply could not get his penis inside me. Even today, after several weeks of trying I still can't let him put more than a small part of his penis into me. I have to have a cushion between us to make sure that he doesn't push it too far into me and I also hold it to make sure that he doesn't push it too far. He wants me to perform oral sex on him but to be honest this is quite impossible.

I have spoken about this to both my sisters and to several lady friends and they all say that they have never heard of a man being so well endowed that he could not fit inside a woman but this really is the case and I would very much appreciate your help.

I have measured my husband's manhood. When limp it is 8 inches long and 6 inches around. When erect it is 14 inches long and 8 inches around.

Large though your husband's penis may be it is still much smaller (and undoubtedly much softer) than the average baby's head and so it should be possible for you to make love properly.

It will, however, probably require some patience, a considerable amount of foreplay and maybe a lubricant to prepare you for sex.

You are also going to have to build up your confidence for I have little doubt that one of the problems now is that when your husband tries to make love to you apprehension and anxiety mean that your muscles contract—making penetration even more difficult.

I think your first step should be to visit your doctor for a check up. It would be wise to check for any infection too since that might make penetration even more painful. While you are there you could ask your doctor to prescribe a suitable lubricant.

Then you should gradually build up your confidence by practising with medically approved artificial objects of gradually increasing size. Your doctor or a gynaecologist should be able to lend you a set of dilators. You should use plenty of lubricant. Be gentle with yourself, don't do anything that hurts and make sure that everything you put inside you comes out again.

When you and your husband are making love you might find it helpful to choose positions where you are in charge. For example, a position in which you are on top will enable you to decide how much of your husband's penis enters you—and at what speed. Take your time and use plenty of lubricant. You may not be able to accommodate the whole of your husband's penis and you should not, of course, do anything that is painful. In the absence of anything else saliva makes a perfectly adequate lubricant and you can choose for yourself how you apply this.

## SPANISH HOLIDAY

Three weeks ago my husband and I went on holiday to Spain. We are both in our early 40s. While we were there we met a young man in his 20s who was on his own. We all spent a lot of time on the beach together and got on well. The young man, who was quite good looking, made no secret of the fact that he was hoping to find a girlfriend for the duration of the holiday but he was completely unsuccessful.

On our last day together I felt so sorry for the young man that while I thought my husband was out water skiing I took him behind a rock, pulled down his swimming trunks and performed oral sex on him. I then let him make love to me. I didn't think my husband had seen any of this but when we were getting changed for dinner that evening he suddenly asked me what the young man and I had been up to on the beach that afternoon.

I tried to pretend that we had just been sunbathing but he told me that he had seen us together. It was no good my trying to blame the young man because my husband had seen me start the whole thing off.

I expected my husband to be angry but he wasn't. He was clearly sexually aroused by the whole experience and he suggested that after dinner I invite the young man back to our room. To cut a long story short the three of us then spent a very exciting night in bed together. I made love to both of them in every imaginable way, both separately and together.

On our way back home my husband told me that he had given the young man our address and telephone number and had invited him to spend the weekend with us. It was pretty clear from the way he told me this that the spare bedroom won't be used. Apparently, while they were in the bar at the airport the young man told him that I was the sexiest woman he had ever been with and provided the best oral sex he had ever had.

My husband also told me that he would like us to find other young men to share our bed. He says he was very turned on by watching me make love to another man.

I now have very mixed feelings about this.

Do you think I should go ahead with my husband's plans or should I stop it now before it goes any further? I have never been the sort of woman who has sexual relations with lots of men and I would not like to have a reputation as an easy woman.

My husband has said that I could say 'no' if he found a man I didn't fancy and he has promised to make sure that any men he brings home are from out of the area.

I can understand you not wanting a reputation as an easy woman, though to be honest I wouldn't have thought women got an awful lot easier than you were in Spain.

Taking a bloke behind some rocks, pulling down his shorts and giving him the kiss of life below the waist doesn't actually put you high on any list of women playing hard to get, does it?

Putting aside the risk of venereal infection (and if you're going to continue with your charitable acts you should make sure that you find a good condom wholesaler) I think you should have a long, hard think about what you want and what you think all this is going to do to your marriage before you go any further.

A one off, spur of the moment sexual adventure on holiday is one thing.

But the sort of organised adultery your husband is talking about is something a little different from the normal.

You need to think about things. And you and your husband need to talk.

I suggest that you put the orgies on hold until you're certain that this is what you really want to do with your life.

......................................................................

## DIVORCED

I am 43 years old and have been divorced for eleven years. During that time I have not had any sort of sexual relationship and to be honest I can't say I really missed sex. I have a responsible job, lots of friends and several time consuming hobbies so my life has been quite busy. Last week all that changed however and I am still in rather a turmoil about what happened. I would appreciate your advice.

Every Tuesday I go swimming and usually do 100 lengths of our local pool. I usually go at around 6.00 pm, straight after work, when it is fairly quiet but last week I was half an hour late and there were quite a few people there who I had never seen before. One of the strangers was a young man, clearly an excellent swimmer. Twice we accidentally bumped into one another in the water. We just apologised to each other and carried on swimming.

Afterwards I popped into the coffee bar and he was there. When he saw me standing at the counter he came over, smiled, apologised again for bumping into me and asked if he could buy me a drink. I said he didn't need to but he was quite insistent and I couldn't see any harm in it so I said yes.

We got talking and found that we had several interests in common. We both play tennis, both like going to the cinema and both enjoy classical music. When he asked me if I'd like to go for a meal with him it seemed perfectly natural to say 'yes' although I insisted that I would pay for myself. I didn't think of it as a 'date'—just two friends going for a meal together.

After we'd eaten I discovered that he didn't have a car so I offered to drive him back to his bed sitting room. When he invited me in for coffee he pointed out that it was still only 10.00 pm so I agreed.

He never did make the coffee. Not until the following morning, at any rate.

To my absolute amazement the moment we got inside his tiny bedsit he asked if he could kiss me. I didn't know what to say because up until that moment I hadn't thought of him as a man—just as a friend. When I felt his body against me I knew that things weren't going to stop there because he was very clearly sexually aroused. He gently put my hand on the front of his trousers and then unfastened my suit jacket with his hands. Less than ten minutes later we were both naked.

I had always assumed that all male penises were much the same sort of size but my new friend's penis was at least twice as large as my former husband's. When I eventually saw it limp I realised that even in that state it was much bigger than my husband's had been erect. I confess that I could not take my eyes off it.

When he took me to bed I was trembling. He asked me what was the matter and I confessed that it had been a long time since I'd made love. I also admitted that I hadn't ever made love to anyone as big as him. I asked him to be very gentle with me and he was. It was a very successful night's love making.

I have seen him twice since then—and spent the night with him both times. He says he loves me and very much wants our relationship to continue. The sex is wonderful (I have even started buying sexy underwear to please him) but it is by no means the only factor in our relationship and I too want it to continue.

I am worried not because he is black (I forgot to mention that) but because he is so much younger than me. I hate to think what people will say when they see us together. I know that some of my friends will disapprove of me. He refuses to tell me his exact age but I don't think he can be more than 22 at the most. What do you think? Should I stop it now before it gets more difficult to stop or should I carry on and see what happens?

What on earth has age got to do with anything? Other people may disapprove but then some people may disapprove of the fact that you are white and he is black. Does it matter? If you are happy with each other then you should enjoy your happiness. Take your pleasure where you will and the future will look after itself. There is little enough joy in this world for any of us. You should not kick happiness aside because of the views of the prejudiced and the narrow minded.

## DULL SEX LIFE

My wife and I have been married for six years and our sex life has got very dull. I think sex is the most important thing in a marriage and so I recently decided that we needed to liven things up a bit. I read in a book that women like being tied up and forced to do things because it liberates them from their feelings of guilt. Last Saturday I got my wife drunk, tied her up and then did several things to her that we had never done before because she wouldn't let me. Even though she was drunk she struggled a lot and she cried afterwards but I've got a very big penis and I think she enjoyed it. Now she says that if I do anything like it again she will leave me. Do you think she is serious or does she really just feel that she has to pretend that she didn't like it? I can't make her out.

Yes, women are difficult to understand aren't they? Sometimes they get very odd and start behaving as though they expect to be treated like real, live human beings. When they find out that they are married to selfish, thoughtless, buttock brained bozos with all the redeeming qualities of gangrene they get upset. What an unpleasant little pustule you are. Incidentally, did you say that you'd got a very large penis or that you were a very large penis? Tell your wife that in my view she should leave you and sue you for every penny you'll ever earn.

## SIX WEEKS

I have been going out with a man for six weeks. We get on very well together. My problem is that I have a two-year-old son from a previous relationship and I am worried that if he finds out he will leave me. Do you think I should tell him now or wait a while?

Tell him now. If you wait any longer then when he finds out he will wonder why on earth you kept such an important secret from him.

## DIRTY WASHING

My boyfriend and I don't live together but he has started to bring his dirty washing round to my flat. Last Saturday he turned up carrying his flat mate's dirty washing as well! I haven't said anything but I feel slightly aggrieved about this. Also, he never cleans his flat and always expects me to do it for him. How can I make it clear that I don't like being used as a slave?

Just put his next batch of dirty washing into a black bag and leave it out with the rubbish. Or you could wash it and take it down to the Oxfam shop. 'Oh, I'm sorry, darling,' you could say, 'I thought you wanted me to give it all to charity.' Or you could try being honest and straightforward

—just tell him how you feel about doing his damned chores! But for heaven's sake do something! If you let things go on the way they are you'll end up feeling bitter and twisted.

····················································

## Party time (£1,000 challenge letter)

My girlfriend and I went to a 21st birthday party recently. The party was held at a hotel which has a swimming pool and after we'd all had quite a bit to drink people started throwing each other into the pool. My best mate and I threw my girlfriend into the water and when she climbed out her strapless dress had slipped right down to her waist. She didn't seem in the slightest bit embarrassed and just took off her sopping wet dress and stood there in her knickers, stockings and suspenders. Before long what had started out as quite a formal party had deteriorated into a semi-nude orgy. Most people were either down to their underwear or were completely naked. I didn't actually have full sex with anyone else but I saw my girlfriend perform oral sex on a man I'd never seen before the party. When I confronted her about it afterwards she said that I could hardly complain since I had been at least partly instrumental in starting the whole thing off. She says she just got carried away. I think there's a lot of difference between throwing someone into the water and performing oral sex on people. What do you think?

I think you're right. There is absolutely no doubt at all there is a lot of difference between throwing someone into a swimming pool and performing oral sex.

You say you didn't actually have 'full sex' with anyone else so I guess it's safe to assume that you didn't stand around admiring the potted plants or picking your finger nails while all this was going on. And since you didn't rush over and interfere when you saw your girlfriend giving a below the belt kiss of life I'd guess that you were involved in a bit of mild hanky panky yourself.

When things get out of control at parties there's always

a tendency to try to apportion blame afterwards. Try to swallow your indignation and not to harbour any hard feelings about your girl friend's errant sperm tasting adventure.

I think your letter is entirely true. A £1,000 personal cheque to you if you can prove me wrong.

............................................................

## SATURDAY LOVERS

My husband can't make love to me for long enough to give me an orgasm. We make love every Saturday night but his erection usually lasts between 3 minutes 15 seconds and 3 minutes 30 seconds. His best time is 4 minutes and even then I didn't have a natural orgasm. We would both appreciate your advice. He has tried wearing two condoms and reciting French verbs to slow him down but nothing seems to work.

I really feel sorry for your husband. In fact I think I might know him. He is a pale, worn out, wasted looking poor devil, isn't he? He spends a lot of time in the pub desperately delaying the time when he has to go home; hoping that by the time he finally arrives you'll have given up waiting, put the watch away and gone to sleep.

I can't get this image out of my mind of your poor old hubby puffing away while you lie there with a stop watch in one hand and a time sheet in the other.

'Je viens huff puff tu viens puff huff il vient huff puff nous venons puff huff vous venez huff puff ils viennent puff huff. Je viens huff puff je viens puff huff je viens!'

In fact, although you obviously don't appreciate his efforts, your husband is really doing quite well: the average human erection doesn't last more than two or three minutes. And since the average female needs three times as long to have an orgasm it is relatively rare for a woman to reach paradise through vaginal sex alone. Most women need a little help.

If you don't want to let your (or his) fingers do the talking may I recommend that you buy one of the new Colchester Climax Pneumatic Petrol Driven 6 Horse Power Vibrators and send your poor old husband off to the knacker's yard. He deserves a more peaceful life and would be undoubtedly be happier if reconstituted as a couple of pints of glue. Alternatively, you could start a serious and meaningful relationship with a ferret. Male ferrets have erections which last up to eight hours.

## DESERTED BEACH (£1,000 CHALLENGE LETTER)

While my wife and I were on holiday we found what we thought was a deserted beach and my wife decided to sunbathe topless. At lunchtime I went back to the car to fetch a book. It was a fifteen minute climb up a cliff path and when I got back to the beach I noticed that two young men in brief swimming trunks were walking across the sands and clearly ogling my wife who hadn't seen them. I should mention that although my wife is in her early 40s she has a terrific figure. Even lying down flat on her back her breasts look like breasts if you know what I mean. My first inclination was to rush over and warn her but for some reason I didn't. Instead I stayed where I was, half hidden behind a rock, and watched. The two men stopped to talk to my wife and then, obviously at her invitation, lay down on the sand next to her. Next, one of the men started kissing her and fondling her breasts. My wife not only let him do this but she then performed a sex act on him and his friend that she will only do for me when she has had several drinks. A few minutes later the two men left. I didn't say anything to my wife about what I'd seen and she didn't mention it either. However, I couldn't hide the fact that I was sexually aroused and right there and then on the beach my wife and I had the best sex we've ever had.

Yours is this week's entry for the Vernon Coleman £1,000 'True or False' Challenge. I don't believe a word of this. What's more you'll have to try much harder than this to gouge £1,000 out of me. The weather in Cornwall in May is far too cold for anyone to lie on a beach unless they are wearing three jumpers and a full set of thermal underwear. But even if it had been boiling hot I wouldn't have believed this letter. It screams 'fake'.

...........................................................................

### EXPENSIVE SEX

My wife makes me pay £10 every time I want to have sex with her. I give her what I think is a generous housekeeping allowance but she says that she doesn't particularly enjoy sex so doesn't see why she shouldn't get something out of it. She spends the money on clothes and at the hairdressers. I say that since I'm paying I'm entitled to choose the way we do it but she will only let me do it in the missionary position.

I can't help feeling that you either have sex a hell of a lot or else your wife buys very cheap clothes. How many frocks can you buy for £10 these days?

I agree with you that you're entitled to choose the way that you have sex with your wife. Since you're paying for sex your physical relationship with your wife has been put on a business footing and you are entitled to have some say over what you get for your money. If she won't budge, and tries to take advantage of her monopoly position, then you should maybe threaten to shop around a little. You might also like to talk about bulk discounts, repeat fees and long term upwards only price reviews. I must say I am terribly impressed by your wife's entrepreneurial instincts. The Government would be proud of her. Privatising all sexual encounters is bound to figure large in their next manifesto. Your wife could, perhaps, apply to be Minister without Knickers.

## BLACK TONGUE

My tongue had got a black coating on it last week. My doctor laughed when I showed it to him. He said it wasn't anything to worry about (I was worried that I'd got cancer) but he didn't say what had caused it. A friend says that cigarette smokers get black tongues but I don't smoke.

You were wise to show your tongue to your doctor. You should always show your doctor any part of your anatomy which changes colour, shape or size and you should never delay in seeking advice. (Having said that, one possible and occasional exception demands a mention: if you are male, it may not be unreasonable to regard sudden, dramatic, temporary and instantly noticeable changes in colour, shape and size as of limited clinical significance when those changes occur as a direct and historically predictable result of sexual arousal and affect an organ which has previously responded in a similar way, and which quickly returns to its original colour, shape and size shortly afterwards as a direct result of stimulating sexual activity. Even in this organ, however, I do stress that you should always seek advice about any changes which seem in any way exceptional, worrying or anything other than temporary.)

I'm glad your doctor was able to reassure you. I'll give you six to four on that you've been taking an antibiotic. Some antibiotics (such as tetracycline) can make your tongue go black by increasing the number of harmless bacteria growing there. If you haven't been taking an antibiotic then I'll give you evens that you've been eating sweets containing liquorice.

## SEXUAL RELIEF

I do not have a girlfriend and have to obtain sexual relief by myself, if you know what I mean. My right wrist (I am right handed) has recently become sore. My doctor said there was nothing seriously wrong with it but asked me if I played any sports which involved a lot of wrist movements. I don't and didn't think of the possible cause until I got home. Do you think the two could be connected?

Yes, I know what you mean and, yes, the two could be connected. It is possible that you could have a unique Repetitive Use Injury. Warn yourself about possible legal action and either train yourself to be ambidextrous or else find someone else to give you a hand occasionally.

........................................................................

## MYSTERY HEADACHES

I suffer a lot from headaches which only started after I took on a new job as a traffic warden. The headaches are always bad at the end of the day. My doctor says they must be stress related but I enjoy my work and do not think this is possible. Do you have any other explanation?

Your nice, shiny new traffic warden's hat could be too small for you. When I was a family doctor I once knew a man whose headaches bewildered some of the nation's top neurologists. Extensive tests showed no abnormalities but in the end we found that his headaches were caused by the fact that he had bought a hat that was too small for him. In medicine the simplest explanations are often the ones which are most difficult to find.

........................................................................

## STILL A VIRGIN

I married when I was 19 and this year I will be 55. I am still a virgin. The first time we tried to make love it hurt and I froze. My doctor sent my husband and me to see a sex therapist but my husband was put off by all the talk of different positions and so on. Gradually, over the years, my husband lost confidence and wouldn't try 'to take me' because he was worried that he would hurt me. Over the years I have had numerous opportunities to have affairs but I never have. I often regret the fact that I haven't ever lost my virginity. We do have a sex life but I do so want to make love properly. Do you think there is any point in seeing a doctor again? I find the prospect of dying a virgin very depressing and rather frightening.

Ring your doctor today and make an appointment to see him or her as soon as you can. You may need a small operation or you may simply need to try using a series of dilators to make your vagina more accessible to your husband's penis. It shouldn't be difficult. I suggest that you say nothing to your husband until you are ready to make love to him. Take your time. Make your virginity a special birthday or Christmas present for him.

........................................................................

## NUDIST

I belong to a family of nudists. My boyfriend does not mind me going to naturist clubs but he won't come with us. It is really quite wearying trying to get him to change his ideas about the subject. How can I tell him that nudism is quite in order?

Why, pray, should he be the one who has to change his views? What about you changing your habits?

I found your attitude just a touch intimidating and I wouldn't be surprised if your boyfriend feels the same way. If you've been brought up to think of it as normal for overweight accountants to barbecue sausages in the nude then nudism probably does seem perfectly natural. The fact is, however, that most of us like to have somewhere to keep our handkerchiefs and whether you like it or not your boyfriend isn't the odd one out—but you are.

I know all the arguments about how healthy it is to wander around without any clothes on but in our society nudism damned well isn't normal and if you want to persuade your boyfriend to wander around without even a posing pouch protecting his little twig and berries then you'll have to be a bit more patient and a hell of a lot more sensitive. Watching a pair of large bosomed women playing an enthusiastic game of nude tennis isn't the sort of thing the average bloke can get accustomed to without a little preparation and a large glass or two of something invigorating.

## YOUNG DAUGHTERS

I have two young daughters and they both suffer a lot from colds, sore throats and ear infections. My doctor won't always give them antibiotics but I think he should. Surely it is dangerous not to treat an infection properly?

There are several reasons why your doctor is right not to prescribe antibiotics every time your children have infections. First, antibiotics won't kill off viruses so prescribing one of these powerful drugs for a cold is a waste of time. Second, antibiotics may be effective but they can be dangerous. It is always wise only to use drugs when they are really needed in order to minimise the risk of unnecessary side effects. You would, I suspect, be pretty upset if one of your daughters had a simple, uncomplicated cold and was made seriously ill by the treatment your doctor had prescribed. Third, if antibiotics are used too often bugs become resistant and can't be killed. This could mean that when your children really need antibiotics the drugs won't work. Fourth, over prescribing antibiotics increases the risk of hypersensitivity or allergy developing.

Please don't be cross if your doctor doesn't think an antibiotic is needed. The human body has a host of in-built defences against infections and sometimes it is best to let those defence systems do the work. Incidentally, I hope you don't mind my mentioning this but because your letter smelt strongly of tobacco I suspect that someone in your house smokes and that could well be the reason why your children suffer so much from ear and throat infections.

When one or both parents smoke babies and young children always seem to catch and be more vulnerable to bugs.

••••••••••••••••••••••••••••••••••••••••••••••••••••••••••••••••

## LIKE A VIRGIN

I am from the East. I lost my virginity recently. I am due to marry soon. It is important that I am a virgin on my wedding night. Is there anything I can do to be like a virgin again? How much does it cost?

There is an operation you can have to restore your virginity; it involves rebuilding your hymen and, if necessary, tightening your vaginal entrance. But if you have only made love a few times there really isn't any need to have such an operation. Your husband will be unlikely to be able to tell that you are not a virgin simply because of the way that you feel when he enters you. Even if he's a doctor and he gives you a full gynaecological examination he won't be able to tell for certain whether or not you are a virgin (assuming you take a few sensible precautions and don't turn up for your examination still hot from your lover's bed).

A century or so ago husbands in the East used to expect their wives to bleed on their wedding night as the hymen was split.

(The hymen, by the way, is a thin sheet of skin across the mouth of the vagina. It usually disappears as a girl grows, leaving only small remnants around the vaginal entrance.)

Proud husbands would then produce the blood stained bedsheets to friends and relatives as evidence that all was well. The absence of any bleeding would, as you suggest, imply that the girl had a less than pure past. However, the fact that brides are often older these days, coupled with the widespread use of tampons and bicycles and the popularity of gymnastics and horse riding among young girls means that very few virgins still have an intact hymen when they get married. Even a routine medical examination can lead to a technical loss of virginity.

Your husband is far more likely to smell a rat as a result of your behaviour rather than as a result of anything he feels. Yelling out 'Do it to me hard!' and wrapping your legs around the small of his back may give the game away. Telling him that you never climax without oral sex or manual stimulation probably isn't a wise move either. I suggest you cry a little. He'll expect sex to be painful for you.

Having said all that I hope you won't mind my asking if you're absolutely sure that this marriage is really what you want? It sounds to me as if you are living in a different world to your husband to be.

••••••••••••••••••••••••••••••••••••••••••••••••••••••••••

## CRAZY ABOUT ME

I have two girl-friends who are both crazy about me. One is a very good looking blonde and our friends all say that we make a really terrific looking couple. The snag with her is that she's a bit thick. The other one isn't all that much to look at but she's devoted to me and will do anything I tell her to do. She's quite a good cook and I think she would make a good housewife. My boss has told me that I won't get promotion at work until I'm married. I'm very tempted to marry the good looking girl (who is slightly the best in bed) but something tells me that maybe the other girl might, in the long run, make a better overall bet. I talked it over with a mate and he said that I should marry the one who would be good around the house because a good pair of legs don't last for ever. I don't want to make a mistake. What do you think I should do?

First, I would like to thank you for writing to me. Since you have honoured me by asking for my advice I'm tempted to tell you that you should get a large pan, fill it with water, put it on the stove and then put your head in it. (Incidentally, you must have a very large head to contain all that conceit so it would obviously need to be a very large pan). Or that you should fill a bath with petrol, sit in it and play with matches. Or that you should take up parachute jumping and get someone with uncontrollable homicidal tendencies to pack your parachute.

But I won't tell you to do any of these things because you are such a moron that you would probably do them and then there would be an inquest and I'd have to go and that would be boring. So *don't* do them. Right?

I would suggest that you buy a plastic blow up doll and marry that but even plastic blow up dolls must have some standards, expectations and rights.

So I suggest that you give up your job and both girl-friends and take up masturbation as a full time career.

You are, after all, already a complete wanker.

## ANIMALS

Why do you care so much about animals? Animals don't have feelings like us. My mate and I go out shooting cats in the evenings because there are so many of them that they're like vermin around where we live. Animal experiments are good because they keep animals under control. Humans are entitled to do what they like with animals because humans are the most important species on earth. And if all the animals in the world had to be wiped out by experimenters so that I could live one day longer I'd think that was great. Animals are like coal and oil; they were put on this earth for us to use.

Like all those who support animal experiments you are clearly a being unencumbered by intellect, compassion or integrity. Your conceit and arrogance and your assumption that as a member of the human race you are inevitably superior to all other creatures reminds me of the abhorrent qualities exhibited by the Nazis. If I had to press a button to decide whether you or a mouse should live the mouse would get my vote. In a decade or so our descendants will look back upon those who now support animal experimentation with revulsion. Morally and ethically, animal experimentation is repugnant. Scientifically and medically animal experimentation is indefensible. Please don't read my column any more. I don't like to think of you reading what I've written.

••••••••••••••••••••••••••••••••••••••••••••••••••••••••••••••••••

## ACROSS THE STREET

I am 42 years old and have lived alone in a terraced house since my mother died. Our street is quite narrow and you can see into the houses across the road quite easily. A few weeks ago I looked out of my bedroom and saw a girl who lives across the street getting changed in her bedroom. The curtains were not drawn and the light was on. She is about 15 and very well developed for her age. Since then I've watched her every morning and evening. Sometimes she wanders around in her underwear for ages. It's a much better show than anything on the TV. She never looks across but I am sure she must know I am watching. I think she wants me to see her. Am I right in thinking that some women get turned on by exposing themselves to men?

You are. But if the 15-year-old girl across the street was deliberately teasing you she would almost certainly look across to check that you were watching. I suspect she's probably just an innocent who doesn't bother to draw the curtains because she doesn't yet realise that she's living opposite a man who's married to his right hand. What you are doing is unhealthy, obsessive and totally reprehensible. Whatever the laws about peeping may be, I dare say there are one or two million men around who would confess that if they caught a glimpse of an attractive neighbour in her undies they wouldn't immediately shield their eyes. But what you're doing falls into a very different category. You are a dirty old man. If you don't stop what you are doing immediately little hairs will grow all over the palms of your hands and you will need to wear spectacles with lenses like milk bottle bottoms. You are this month's recipient of the Vernon Coleman Grubby Raincoat Award. Your prize is a curse: May the zip on your fly always catch on your tender bits.

## Party Trick

Two weeks ago while we were fooling around in a hotel bedroom my husband picked up my handbag and hung it on his erect penis. Since then he's done this several times and it has become a sort of 'party trick'. He keeps putting more and more things into the bag and is now threatening to do it next time we have visitors. I'm worried that he may damage himself permanently because presumably the penis isn't built for carrying around heavy weights.

The load bearing capacity of the erect human penis is around 5 to 6 pounds but this is generally regarded as a theoretical capacity rather than a practical capability.

It is not unusual for the penis to be used as a stage prop for circus tricks. For example, hoopla is regarded as an entertaining alternative in some areas and participants use old bicycle tyres, doughnuts or polo mints depending upon the circumference of the target.

I strongly advise against any such activity. The erect penis is a delicate and sensitive piece of equipment which should be treated with care and respect at all times.

## Well Off

Before we married my husband was always spending money on me. I thought he was really well off. I was wrong. It was only after the wedding that I discovered just how much debt he was in. In an attempt to help pay off the debts I got a job as a bar maid in a nightclub. After a few weeks the manager told me that some of the customers would pay to have a girl spend the evening with them and that he thought I could do the job. He told me that all I had to do was to keep them happy and to try to get them to spend as much as possible on drink. At the end of the first evening, when my customer asked me to go back to his hotel with him, I was rather shocked. I refused but the man gave me a tip anyway. Since then I have continued to work as a hostess. I don't and won't go to bed with any of the men but I let them kiss me and fondle me because the tips are better. Sometimes I feel guilty but it is my husband's fault that we are in debt and he still spends our money on extravagant things that we don't really need. Do you think that what I am doing is wrong? I haven't told my husband what my job entails but I'm pretty sure he has more or less guessed. After all I take home far more than I did as a bar maid. I guess he knows as well as I do that it's the only way we that we can support our lifestyle.

No, I don't think that what you are doing is wrong. Working for a tobacco company is wrong. Mugging old ladies is wrong. Working for a company that passes a mixture of chemicals, water and ground up intestines off as 'sausage' is wrong. Working for a lawyer who helps drug companies avoid their responsibilities is wrong. Writing TV ads designed to persuade kids to pressurise their parents into buying expensive crap is wrong. Dressing up, getting on a horse and chasing foxes and stags around the countryside is wrong. Falsifying evidence so that innocent people go to prison is wrong.

Put what you do in perspective and the guilt should melt away. You and your husband are the only people likely to be hurt by what you do for a living so if you can live with it I'm damned sure the rest of us can.

Allowing a few tired businessmen to squeeze your tits might not be the sort of job careers guidance teachers get excited about but there are several million people doing jobs which make you like look Mother Teresa.

. . . . . . . . . . . . . . . . . . . . . . . . . . . . . . . . . . . . . . . . . . . . . . . . . . . . . . . . . .

## FANTASY

My husband were recently discussing our sex fantasies. He confessed that he had always wanted to watch two women making love. I admitted that it was something I had long wanted to experience myself. We said no more about it but the thought wouldn't go away. Lat week I saw a TV programme about prostitutes in Amsterdam. These girls are checked regularly by a doctor. As my husband's birthday is coming up I am thinking of taking him to Amsterdam for a weekend and letting him watch me and another girl make love. Please tell me if you think there is any reason why I should not do this.

I hate to be the voice of caution but you ought to talk to your husband a bit more about this before you buy the plane tickets.

I admire the thought—letting your husband watch you go dutch in a shop window in Amsterdam sounds more fun than buying him a new power drill or a soap on a rope—but there are several reasons for my reluctance to cheer you on unreservedly.

First, there is a big difference between what people fantasise about and what they're prepared to do in real life. Your husband's heart might start doing somersaults if he suddenly finds himself enjoying a ringside seat at a two woman show where you enjoy joint star billing. One of the joys of a fantasy is that there are no messy consequences. Real life isn't always quite so neat.

Second, the risk you run of contracting an infection may be fairly low but it isn't non existent. Sexually transmitted diseases can be passed on during lesbian encounters.

Third, what are you going to do if you find that you enjoy your lesbian adventure more than you have ever enjoyed sex with your husband? You're going to be performing with a professional. She'll know what buttons to press to turn you into a quivering jelly. Turning your fantasy into reality could change your lives. One or both of you might end up wishing you'd stuck to the soap on a rope.

All things considered I don't think this is the sort of gift you should keep as a surprise. Next time you're talking dirty with your husband tell him about your idea and see how he reacts. If he gets indignant you can always tell him that you were just pushing the fantasy a little bit further. If he agrees you can get him to go dutch.

● ● ● ● ● ● ● ● ● ● ● ● ● ● ● ● ● ● ● ● ● ● ● ● ● ● ● ● ● ● ● ● ● ● ● ● ● ● ● ● ● ● ● ●

## LONG HAIR

I work as a stylist in a women's hairdressing salon and for several months I have had a problem. Every time I have to work on a client who has very long hair I get an erection. None of my clients ever realise this, of course, and I have recently taken to wearing a loose shirt outside my trousers to hide the evidence but I am beginning to get concerned. Is this as unusual as I fear it is, does it mean that I am a pervert and what can I do about it? One busy day just before Christmas I had an erection for six hours. I rang my girlfriend to come round and help me out but she was too busy and I think she thought I'd gone potty. If I knew it was normal I wouldn't mind but I don't like to think that I'm turning into some sort of sex monster.

Lots of men find women's hair a sexual turn on and long hair is more likely to be sexually stimulating than short hair. You certainly aren't a pervert.

Apart from buying baggy trousers or specialising in women with short hair I don't really think there is much you can do about this; though you could visit a psychologist and get yourself deconditioned.

The simplest solution might be to find a quiet spot, ring your girlfriend and dispose of the evidence as soon as it comes up.

I wonder if your problem might not be commoner than the public realise. Could it be that this explains why so many male hair stylists walk funny?

Perhaps women having their hair done by stylists in long shirts or overalls should watch their backs in future.

● ● ● ● ● ● ● ● ● ● ● ● ● ● ● ● ● ● ● ● ● ● ● ● ● ● ● ● ● ● ● ● ● ● ● ● ● ● ● ● ● ● ● ●

## HOW SAFE?

For four years my husband and I have slept regularly with a male friend who has sex with us both. Is this safe?

Serious risks are low if the three of you are free of any sexually transmitted diseases and if none of you has or has had sex with any other partners.

But there are still risks.

For example, if your friend makes love to your husband using his back passage (the one he keeps in his trousers not the one where he keeps his bicycle) and then makes love to you using your front passage (the one you keep in your knickers, not the one where you keep the carved wooden umbrella stand and the barometer from Spain) there is a risk that you will become infected. You can minimise this particular hazard by using fresh condoms for each Act in your evening's entertainment.

I could probably think of a dozen slightly bizarre ways in which your *ménage à trois* could damage your health but all this is just too much for me and I'm off now to lie down in a darkened room.

Incidentally, do you have a rota for making the tea in the morning?

· · · · · · · · · · · · · · · · · · · · · · · · · · · · · · · · · · · · · · · · · · · · · · · · · · · · · · · ·

## BROAD MINDED

My fiancé and I have a satisfying love life but he is constantly trying to persuade me to have sex in different positions. I am very broad minded but I don't see the point in all this experimentation since we can both reach orgasms perfectly satisfactorily in the missionary position. Some of the positions he has suggested are very rude and suggestive. He also wants me to wear some sexy clothes he has bought me but this seems rather dirty. I don't see the point in this anyway since although I do occasionally let him leave the light on we are obviously always in bed when we make love and so he wouldn't be able to see anything I was wearing. I am beginning to think that he may be a pervert.

Your boyfriend doesn't sound like a pervert but you sound like a prude. You certainly aren't as broad minded as you like to think you are. In a nunnery or at an editorial meeting of some newspapers you might possibly be considered broad minded. Out here in the real world you're not.

Why do you have sex? If you do it because you want to get pregnant then I quite agree with you that there's no need to experiment with different positions. If all the equipment is functioning properly you can lie flat on your back, he can slide up and down a few times and then you can both groan, roll over, go to sleep and contentedly dream of lawn care and soft furnishings.

However, if you have sex for the only other reason—because it's fun—then experimenting will make it more fun. If you constantly ate the same meals, listened to the same music and watched the same movies on TV then life would soon get pretty dreary wouldn't it? Variation adds spice.

You may find this surprising (in fact I think you'd better sit down and hold onto something firm) but quite a lot of perfectly ordinary, sensible people make love out of bed. They do it on the living room floor, on the kitchen table and even in the park. What's more they look at and touch each other's bodies—sometimes naked and sometimes partly clothed in sensual and erotic underwear—while they're doing it. A recent survey of smiling women showed that 95% preferred sexual positions that could most accurately be described as rude or suggestive.

I think you've got some exciting times ahead of you. Listen to your fiancé, enjoy the educational experience that awaits and before long you'll be ready to take your 'Ooh!' and 'Aah!' level exams.

········································································

## GOOD NEIGHBOURS

I am in my fifties and since my wife does not enjoy the best of health our sex life is non existent. To obtain relief I masturbate in the garden shed while looking at pictures of naked ladies. The shed is right at the bottom of my garden. A few months ago I inadvertently left the shed door slightly ajar and looked up to see that the woman who lives next door (who is in her late forties) was standing watching me. Since then every time I have gone into the shed my neighbour has gone into her garden and watched. Recently she has taken to stooping down in such a position that I can see that she is not wearing any panties. I feel a great deal of guilt after each of these sessions but I cannot stop myself.

And why should you stop yourself? You aren't doing anyone any harm. You're just a lonely, harmless rake in a garden shed. Leaving the shed door open could have got you into trouble if the neighbour's gnome had seen your garden tool and called in the social workers. But solitary manual labour is nothing to feel bad about and the fact that you have attracted an obviously appreciative audience is more a tribute to your natural skills than a cause for anguish. Your relationship with the woman next door is not exactly usual but I don't think you should lose any sleep over the fact that you are both now members of the same Neighbourhood Watch scheme.

## BEAUTIFUL GIRL

For five weeks I have been going out with the most beautiful girl I have ever seen. She is the prettiest, most delicate, most feminine, most loving and most charming woman I've ever known. She is incredible in bed. She loves sex in every possible position and nothing I have ever suggested has surprised or shocked her.

Two nights ago she turned my world upside down and inside out by telling me that she started out her life as a man. She confessed that she had a sex change operation in her early twenties. She said she told me because she loves me and was terrified that I would find out from someone else.

I was (and am) absolutely stunned. I just don't know what to do or say. There are so many things I want to ask her (for example: did she have sex before she had her sex change operation and if so did she make love to men or women?). But I'm not at all sure that I can cope with the answers. Part of me wants to run and never see her again. But part of me is very much in love with her. What do I do?

I can, I think, just about comprehend your confusion. It must have been quite a shock to find out that your girlfriend might once have been someone else's boyfriend.

I don't think you should do anything rash. I don't think you should leave her. And I don't think you should ask her to share your underwear drawer just yet. I think you should give yourself time.

I suspect that your girlfriend will understand that you need time to think. She, after all, has had a lifetime to get accustomed to her double sexual identity.

My guess is that once you've got over the shock—and you've asked and she's answered all the tricky questions— you'll want to stay with her. She is, after all, still the most beautiful girl you've ever seen. And still the most loving, charming and delicate woman you've ever met. History doesn't change any of that. The fact that she now sits down to do what she once did standing up should make no real difference to your relationship.

······································································

## DEEPLY ATTRACTED

I am 59 years old and am deeply attracted to a man I work with. He is single and unattached but twenty years my junior. He seems to enjoy my company and I think he would like to continue our friendship outside working hours. So far I have gently dissuaded him from any move in this direction (i.e. I have steered the conversation onto other ground when I have felt that he's been about to invite me out) simply because I am very conscious of our age difference. Do you think I am right to be cautious? He knows my age but I don't want to be hurt by starting a relationship which is doomed because of our age difference. On the other hand I would like to go out with him.

For heaven's sake let the poor guy ask you out. And if, in the fullness of time, he wants to hold your hand, and maybe even initiate skin contact of a more intimate nature, encourage him. What are you waiting for? Reincarnation?

Life is full of potential misery. Around every corner there is a traffic warden waiting to sticker your car, a lawyer waiting to stick a writ into your hand and a white coated scientist waiting to describe a new cause of cancer. Happiness, joy and the pleasures of the flesh should be welcomed with open arms at every opportunity.

## TRIVIA

My husband and I stay in every night and do nothing but sit slumped in our chairs watching TV. I can almost feel my brain and body rotting. My mind is filled with trivia. The other day a friend I hadn't seen for years rang up and I couldn't wait to get her off the phone because I was watching a television programme. Afterwards I felt depressed about what is happening to me. Why did I give the TV precedence over my friend? I'd like to do other things but my husband says that everyone stays in these days. I can't face spending the rest of my life this way.

There is still time for you to save yourself, though I fear that there is no hope for your husband. He has become an intellectual no-go area; a cathode ray dullard; as exciting as a string vest and with about as much hope for the future as an unadopted road.

Start going out in the evenings. Enrol at a night school. Join the library. Take up pottery or aerobics. Learn the tango. Join a belly dancing group. Get a part time job as a strippergram girl. Join a political group and start plotting the government's downfall. Do anything—but make sure that you get out of your flat before you start finding yourself genuinely concerned about next week's TV programmes. Leave the boring gaseous waste you are married to with a flask of sweet tea and the remote control device and he probably won't even notice that you've escaped.

## FOREIGN OBJECTS

My husband is constantly begging me to let him put a variety of objects inside me—bananas, cucumbers, candles, roll on deodorant stick. If I refuse we have an argument and he sulks. I wouldn't mind if he wanted to do these things as part of love making—but to him I'm just a sex object. He took topless photos of me and although he promised not to show anyone he had shown them to a friend within two days. He made a video of us making love and, again, took the tape round to show his friend. I would love to leave him but I have nowhere to go.

Sex games have to be fun and both partners have to be willing. Otherwise they aren't games. Your husband is simply using and abusing you and he sounds about as much fun as herpes. Encourage your husband to keep doing the shopping by telling him that he hasn't yet brought home anything to which you really fancy making love. Soon your house will be stocked entirely with phallic shaped groceries and toiletries. But you will have been able to save the housekeeping money. And within six months you should be able to tell the pathetic old fool the location of another secret burial place for his collection of fruit, vegetables and roll on deodorants.

## NO INTIMACY

My boyfriend is very cold and distant towards me. We have been together for several years now but things seem to be getting worse. The only time he touches me is when we are in bed and even then it is never loving or affectionate but is more a dutiful prelude to sex. When it is over there is no intimacy or afterplay. Sometimes without any warning he just jumps on me without any show of affection or foreplay beforehand. He doesn't talk to me and often ignores me for hours. This is all making me feel taken for granted and I feel that I will soon lose my confidence. I am slim with a great figure and a wacky sense of humour and I get offers from men all the time yet my boyfriend hardly seems to notice that I'm there. I need more warmth and tenderness. For me the biggest turn on of all would be just feeling that my boyfriend really wanted me.

You are right: you are being taken for granted! You need to remind your boyfriend how much you love him and persuade him to remember how much he loves you. Suggest a romantic weekend away together. Buy yourself some obscenely erotic underwear and let him catch an occasional, teasing glimpse of milky white thigh or gently heaving bosom. Try flirting gently with one or two of your admirers when he's around. Send him flowers and champagne. Turn up at the place where he works, throw your arms around his neck and ask him if he still loves you. Write him a long, provocative love letter and arrange an assignation in a nearby romantic hotel. Cook his favourite meal, light the table with candles and wear a French maid outfit to serve the food. Buy yourself a nightie that weighs less than a breathless whisper. If all that fails I should have him checked out because he may well not be human.

●●●●●●●●●●●●●●●●●●●●●●●●●●●●●●●●●●●●●●●●●●●●●●●●●●●●●●●●●●●

## TIED UP

My boyfriend and I were fooling around recently and ended up with me flat on my back on the bed with him lying on top of me. To stop me wriggling he was using one hand to hold my hands together above my head. He then kissed me and started to unfasten the buttons down the front of the shirt I was wearing with his free hand. Finding this difficult to do he pulled out his pyjamas from underneath the pillow. He used one leg of the trousers to tie my left hand to the bed head and one arm of his jacket to tie my other hand to the right hand side of the bedhead. When he had finished tying me up he finished unfastening my shirt and pushed my bra up so that he could kiss my breasts. He clearly found it very exciting to have me tied up in this way. I confess that I was excited by it too. He pushed up my skirt, pulled my knickers and tights down to my knees and made love to me quite aggressively. It was all quite spontaneous and afterwards we both agreed that it had been very exciting. I was quite surprised to find that I enjoyed not having any control over what was happening to me. Is this sort of sex very kinky? I'd like to do it again and my boyfriend has admitted that he would like me to tie him up next time.

Having sex while one of you is tied up is neither unusual nor kinky. It's very common. An entirely unreliable recent survey showed that 72% of citizens do this at least once a week. If a secretary tells you that her boss is tied up she probably means it. Both women and men confess that they enjoy it. Remember that bondage is not about hurting and it should only ever be done with the consent of both partners. Make sure that the knots can always be quickly and easily undone (by the person who is tied up if necessary) and don't ever tie anything around anyone's neck. Don't get into bondage after drinking alcohol and always arrange some sort of code so that if the person who is tied up wants to be released she or he can communicate this information in a way that will be understood. Yelling: 'Stop it, oh, stop it you beast!' isn't always taken at face value in these circumstances.

## SHOUTING

I have started shouting at my wife and children a lot. I know I'm doing it but knowing about it only seems to make things worse. I get irritable and cross with myself about the fact that I'm short tempered and the end result is that I shout and nag even more. I really don't know what to do to change myself. I suspect that problems at work are the main cause of my bad temper.

The most straightforward solution would be to direct your anger towards the people who are upsetting you. Next time you find yourself thwarted by a spotty sixteen-year-old in a suit or a geriatric and possibly incontinent buffoon share your feelings with them. What's the worst that can happen if you speak your mind? Is losing a job that is messing up your life really such a disaster? Next time someone at work upsets you imagine that you're talking to a four-year-old who's just left his damned skate board in the middle of the driveway for the fourteenth time in a week. Get the blood pumping into the veins on your temples, grit your teeth and start spitting insults. If anyone whinges explain to them that you've received advice that keeping in your feelings is dangerous to your health.

If for some reason or other you feel shy about doing verbal damage at work then find a physical outlet for your anger. Check with your doctor first (to make sure that you aren't likely to do yourself any permanent damage), warn your wife that you're going to be late but that you aren't having an affair with the big bosomed receptionist who always smiles at you, and then call in at a gym or sports centre on the way home and swim a few lengths, batter a squash ball flat or pedal five miles on a stationary bicycle. By the time you've showered and dressed and driven home you should be nicely mellow.

## MISSIONARY

Can you please tell me what the missionary position is? I am a 25-year-old girl and am getting married at Christmas.

To adopt the missionary position for sex you should lie flat on your back with your legs slightly apart. Your fiancé then lies on top of you. If the two of you are of roughly equal height you can kiss and have sex at the same time. If he is much shorter than you are then he can kiss your breasts (with your permission, of course) while you examine the ceiling and try and decide whether it would look nicer in mushroom, grey gloss or cornflower blue in a matt finish. If he is much taller than you then he can slobber on the pillow while you nuzzle his neck. This position, one of the perennial favourites with most couples, got its name when two missionaries visited the South Sea Islands a long time ago. The islanders, who didn't have television and were consequently rather imaginative in their love making, laughed when they saw the two missionaries dutifully carrying out the physical aspect of their marriage in the position I have described.

........................................................................

## TURNED DOWN

My daughter, who is 26 years old, was bitterly disappointed to be turned down for a job. She found out that she had been rejected because the medical form filled in by her doctor disclosed that she had once taken an overdose. According to the personnel officer of the company concerned she was turned down because she was considered 'mentally unstable'. Will this always go against her? It was an isolated incident which happened after an unhappy love affair.

This sort of thing happens a lot. At least your daughter found out what had happened. Most people never find out why they were rejected. The truth is, of course, that if everyone who had ever exhibited any sign or symptom of being 'mentally unstable' was turned down for employment then no one would be working. Personnel Officers (or Human Resource Management Executives as they pompously like to be addressed these days) have a tendency to rely on preprinted forms prepared in 1922 when hiring new staff and don't seem to have realised yet that anyone who hasn't felt so pissed off with the world that they occasionally think of the ultimate goodbye is probably insensitive, thick skinned and blessed with about as much compassion as a traffic bollard. As you and your daughter have realised, the problem is that once an example of apparent mental instability is reported on a medical record it is very difficult to get it removed. And if your daughter refuses to allow prospective employers to contact her doctor they will doubtless be convinced that she is a psychotic, psoriatic social psychopath with tuberculosis, halitosis, leprosy and a tendency to vomit uncontrollably over strangers. Apart from stealing and doctoring her medical records the only answer is for your daughter to be totally honest when applying for work and to throw herself on the mercy of the person doing the hiring. Eventually she will probably find some daring and magnanimous soul who will enjoy the glow of self satisfaction to be obtained by hiring her.

## UNUSUAL FANTASY

While having sex with my husband I don't fantasise about other men like I know a lot of women do. Instead I fantasise about my husband having sex with other women. This really turns me on although I know I wouldn't want him to do it in real life. He knows about my fantasy and tells me what he would like to do them. Sometimes we fantasise together about real women we both know. Are there any other women like me?

Yes. An entirely unreliable survey conducted recently showed that 72% of women with breasts of A cup size or larger regularly fantasised about their husbands making love to other women. There are absolutely no rules in fantasy land. No rights, no wrongs and no need ever to feel guilty. Fantasising is healthy and much cheaper, less troublesome and more effective than psychoanalysis. You can get rid of hidden fears, hopes, and guilts through sexual fantasies. You can exorcise unidentified ghosts and enjoy yourself without worrying about boundaries or what the neighbours will say. It is particularly wonderful that you and your husband can share a fantasy world. And it must be quite fun to be able to listen to your husband's wild and unbridled fantasies about that pompous woman in tweeds who always talks as though she's got her mouth full and walks as though she's got a prize winning courgette stuck up her bum.

........................................................................

### STUNNED

My younger sister was depressed last year after having a baby. While she was feeling low she did a lot of comfort eating and put on a lot of excess weight. I persuaded her to join a slimming club and arranged for my 19-year-old daughter to baby sit for her. A few days ago I found myself at a loose end so I decided to pop round and join my daughter. I walked round to the back door and glanced in through the window before I knocked. I was stunned to see her kissing my brother in law. It wasn't a casual kiss. He was undoing her blouse and she had her hand on his trousers. I rushed off feeling sick and sat in my car for a while. When I went back I rang the front door bell. It was quite a while before anyone answered and both my daughter and my sister's husband looked very guilty and flustered. I didn't say anything at the time and now I don't know what to do. Should I tell my daughter, my son in law or my sister? I have no one to talk to you except you. I can hardly bear to look at my daughter and I know she is wondering why I am so quiet and withdrawn.

I don't think you should say anything to your son in law or your sister. Their marriage is their affair and neither of them will thank you for interfering. If you say anything to your daughter she'll probably accuse you of being an inter-fering mother or of spying on her or of both. I think you should wait a while. With any luck she'll ask you what's worrying you and then, under pressure, you can tell her what you saw, explain that you are naturally concerned but make it clear that you are well aware that it has nothing to do with you and you aren't making any moral judgements. By taking a fairly neutral stance and making it clear that although you are concerned you aren't being judgemental you will leave the way open for your daughter to talk to you if she feels she needs a sympathetic, friendly ear.

## SUCKER

I like sucking my wife's breasts. Although she hasn't been pregnant for several years she still produces milk which I drink. Will this do me any harm?

This habit is unlikely to harm you unless you do it in public in which case it may affect your credibility if you run for political office.

## ROWS

I am having terrible rows with my thirteen-year-old daughter. She disagrees with everything I say and some of the rows we have are frighteningly fierce. I have never known anything like it before and it frightens me.

I'm sorry. I only give advice about how to deal with human relationships. Teenagers do not fit into this category. I can only suggest that you hold firm and try to stay calm. The crisis you are going through will resolve itself in around six years. If things get really bad clench your fists, stamp your feet and shout.

## LOST CONTACT

I wear contact lenses and like to go swimming. Twice
recently I have lost a lens while diving into the pool. Can
you give me any advice on how to avoid this problem? I
don't want to have to give up diving.

Shut your eyes when diving or jumping into the water
(after making sure that you aren't going to land on
anyone). Or wear goggles. Or you can get larger lenses
which are less likely to come out.

## WORK LOAD

I have been trying for years to cut down my work-load. But
the older I get the more impossible I seem to find it to catch
up with the chores I'm supposed to do. I never have time
for any fun any more. How can I organise my life better?

I know how you feel. I use nine (yes, nine) desks and
they're always overflowing. But although none of us likes
to admit it, the truth is that much of what we all do is
crap—forms to fill in, bills to pay, circulars to file in the bin,
cock ups by big organisations to put right, complaints to
make, solicitors' letters to throw away. The only answer is
to be firm with yourself and make having fun one of your
priorities.

We are all taught from childhood that work must take
precedence over everything else we do and that we must
finish our chores before we even think of having any fun.
Long ago someone (probably a podgy Victorian mill owner
with an under-developed sense of fun and an over-devel-
oped sense of greed) invented the concept of 'work before
pleasure'. Millions of us have been stupid enough to let this
saying rule our lives. It took me several decades to realise
that since there will always be work to do following this
philosophy can mean a life quite devoid of pleasure.

Take your pleasures seriously. Plan them into your life. Without regular fun you will become tired, ratty, inefficient, unimaginative and ineffective. And when it's funtime ignore the phone, abandon the crap on your desk, leave the washing up and the weeds in the garden and go and have fun.

(I'm off to the beach in a minute).

......................................................

## QUIETLY IN LOVE

I have been married for twelve years to a kind and gentle man who has always treated me with respect and who has given me two small children and a lovely home. Materially I have everything a woman could reasonably ask for. But for six years I have been quietly in love with someone else. From things he has said I know that he feels the same about me. Despite our feelings we have never made love or even kissed one another, though we see each other quite often and live near to one another. I would never dream of leaving my family but as I get older I am beginning to feel that I would very much like to have an affair. My husband is not particularly romantic and our sex life, which was never very spectacular, is now more or less non existent. I don't want to die with what might have been the big love of my life nothing more than a regret.

If you want me to tell you that it's OK to have an affair then I'm afraid you're going to be disappointed. You have to take that awesome decision yourself. But think things through carefully before you take the plunge. If you start an affair can you keep it secret? Will you be able to cope with the guilt? And are you sure that you will be satisfied with a love affair? The downside of having an affair is that you could wreck your marriage and end up with nothing. On the other hand you could find out that the man you think you are in love with is a boring, unimaginative lover who wears baggy white Y fronts and thinks oral sex is something that women do for men—and that knowledge might make you feel far more content with your marriage. The downside of not having an affair is that you will never know the excitement of having one. And unless you try him out you'll never know what sort of lover your dream man might turn out to be. Whatever you choose to do there will be times when you will have regrets so if you choose to have an affair make sure that you know what you are doing. And don't forget that even grown ups have to watch out for diseases and unwanted pregnancies.

## VIBRATOR ADDICT

I am addicted to my vibrator. I used to masturbate with my fingers but after I discovered the vibrator I abandoned this method. My boyfriend says that regular use of the vibrator may damage my reproductive organs and that I should stop using it. Is there any truth in this?

It depends entirely on what you do with it. If you use the vibrator to stimulate your clitoris then your reproductive organs are unlikely to be affected. Maybe your boyfriend is simply jealous of the fact that a piece of plastic with a battery in it has already given you more orgasms than he could hope to give you in a lifetime of enthusiastic love making. And maybe you should listen to him. Your vibrator may be efficient but it won't be much good when you want a cuddle.

## CHRISTMAS PARTY

I am dreading going to my husband's annual Christmas party because his boss is a lecher and I hate him pawing me. Every year he moves around the room during the dinner, doing what I think he feels is a regal walkabout. He always gropes and paws any woman he finds attractive. Last year he stood behind me, peering down my cleavage, and slid the straps of my dress down over my shoulders. I just managed to catch my dress before my nipples were exposed. I tried to slap him but missed and afterwards my husband told me off. He said that I could have damaged his prospects of promotion. Later the boss insisted on dancing with me and kept squeezing my bottom. He took great delight in pushing a very obvious erection against me.

I asked my husband if I could stay at home this year but he says all wives are expected to go and that if I don't it will be a black mark against him.

Tell your husband that you'll go to his sordid little 'do' if he insists but that if Caligula lays a finger on you then you'll deck him. (Alternatively, if you don't want to risk spoiling your nails, tell him that you'll toss a glass of wine— preferably red because the stains are more obvious—over the malodorous little squirt).

If your husband had any balls he would have done this himself at last year's party but from the way the boss behaves I suspect that the company either has a policy of employing only eunuchs or else makes orchidectomy an essential part of the internal orientation programme.

................................................................

## CRUSH

I am a 36-year-old divorced woman and for some time I have known that my son's 15-year-old friend has got a crush on me. Recently, while my son was visiting his father, this boy called round. We were sitting on the sofa when he suddenly blurted out that he found me very beautiful and wanted to kiss me. I felt in control of the situation and so I let him.

However, things got out of hand and he charmed me out of my clothes and into bed. I was amazed at how satisfied he left me. I made him promise not to breathe a word to anyone but I am ashamed of myself. I have got a feeling that he will want to repeat this and I know that he could make things difficult should I refuse him. I truly regret what happened.

If you have sex with him again because you are frightened of what he might say then you'll be even more vulnerable to blackmail. If you really do regret what happened then you should try to avoid being alone with him. If he manages to proposition you again tell him how wonderful sex with him was but point out that although you'd love to repeat the experience you don't feel that you can. Be firm but let him down lightly, and make sure he knows that you're flattered and that you found him an excellent lover. Finally, it sounds to me as if you really need to find yourself a more legally acceptable lover. The fact that you allowed a 15-year-old to charm you out of your knickers suggests that you're rather over-ripe for plucking. Get out more and find yourself a lover over 16 before you find yourself trying to explain how you were charmed out of your clothes and into your bed by your 11-year-old paperboy.

## BICYCLE ACCIDENT

When my girlfriend and I had sex for the first time there was no bleeding. When I asked her why, she said that she had an accident on her bicycle. My friend says this is impossible and that all women bleed the first time they have sex if they are virgins. We are supposed to get married soon.

Well, your friend the expert doesn't know as much as he thinks he knows about gynaecology. He should stick to weather forecasting, sending out electricity bill demands, running his local police force or doing whatever other dreary and undemanding occupation normally fills his dozy days. The use of tampons and the widespread popularity of bicycles, horses and gymnastics mean that it is now commonplace for there to be no sign other than a cry of surprise or disappointment to mark the magic moment when a girl becomes a woman.

More importantly, may I ask what the hell you were

doing discussing your fiancée's virginity with your little friend? When did you do this—during the milk break at school? Gentlemen don't share such confidential titbits with their chums. At least they don't if they're English.

If your girlfriend tried to hide the truth from you then this was probably because she knew that you would disapprove if you knew that she had had sex with someone else. But why do you disapprove? Surely what really matters is not who your girlfriend had sex with before she met you but who she has sex with in the future. If you love her it shouldn't matter if she's had sex with the entire national army, all politicians and the local church choir.

••••••••••••••••••••••••••••••••••••••••••••••••••••••••••••

## A CERTAIN WEEKEND

A good friend has asked me to lie for him. If his wife asks, he wants me to confirm that he was with me on a certain weekend last month. He has apparently told her that he was with me because he spent the weekend with another woman. What on earth should I do?

L ie. If you think of it as helping to save his marriage rather than giving him an alibi for his philandering. And if you feel uncomfortable about it, tell him that while you'll do it this time you won't do it again.

••••••••••••••••••••••••••••••••••••••••••••••••••••••••••••

## PUBIC TRIM

My husband wants to trim my pubic hair. He saw a picture of a girl whose pubic hair had been cut into a heart shape and he wants to do the same to me. Is this unusual or perverted? Can it do me any harm? Will my pubic hair grow back if it is cut?

A s long as he doesn't suffer from delirium tremens there is no need for you to worry. Pubic hair styling is now extremely fashionable and I have it on the best authority that some very regal curly bits have been subjected to the stylist's scissors (for heaven's sake don't tell anyone else—I don't think this is supposed to be public knowledge). Knowing that there is many a neatly clipped bikini bush nestling beneath a pair of skimpies I often wonder which public figures have yet taken the plunge—and what style they have chosen. Finally, if your very own Mr Snip makes a botch of things and you end up bald you need not worry too much. Your pubic hair will grow back again quite quickly—though it will, I'm afraid, be rather itchy for a while and so your husband could, for the first time, be the one complaining of a razor rash.

· · · · · · · · · · · · · · · · · · · · · · · · · · · · · · · · · · · · · · · · · · ·

## BACK ENTRANCE

I have been going with my present partner for several years. Our sex life is very good but some time ago while we were having sex she withdrew my penis and put it into her anus. I was rather embarrassed at the time but didn't show it. Since then she has done this on numerous occasions. She seems to enjoy it very much. Is it dangerous?

Anal sex is far more common than you might imagine. Men sometimes find it enjoyable because the entrance is tighter. Some women claim it gives them a more intense orgasm. Unfortunately, anal sex is the best method of sex for transmitting AIDS.

· · · · · · · · · · · · · · · · · · · · · · · · · · · · · · · · · · · · · · · · · · ·

## COLD BUM

I suffer from a cold bum. I am 66 years old. My doctor says my circulation is excellent.

Wear warmer knickers. Congratulations on reaching such a good age despite the coolness of your rear. And look on the bright side. If your freezer ever packs up you can keep your food cold by sitting on it.

## QUITE A SHOCK

When I went to bed with my current boyfriend for the first time I had quite a shock. I discovered that he wears ladies knickers underneath his trousers. He said he got into the habit of doing this when he borrowed a pair of a former girlfriend's panties after he'd fallen into a swimming pool. He insisted that he isn't a transvestite or bisexual. Have you heard of other men doing this?

Your boyfriend isn't gay. The sale of baggy white underpants has been badly affected in recent years as thousands of perfectly heterosexual men have decided that knickers intended for women feel much nicer and are sexier to wear. Many heterosexual men have discarded their Y fronts and boxer shorts in favour of silky panties.

How can I be so sure about your boyfriend? Simple. Your boyfriend's openness about his preference is a sign that he feels confidently heterosexual.

## HOMEWORK

I spend an hour and a half doing my homework every evening and nearly always get quite good marks. I concentrate hard and work as quickly as I can so that I can get everything done as quickly as possible. My parents say that if I spent longer on my homework I would get better marks. They may be right but if I spent more time on my homework I'd have to give up my aerobic classes, my dancing, my hockey and singing in a local choir. My parents say I should concentrate exclusively on my schoolwork so that I get the best possible marks. What do you think? They'll listen to you because they trust your judgement.

School teachers and parents have created endless misery by accepting the myth that we should all do everything we do to the very best of our ability. That damned silly phrase 'If a thing is worth doing it is worth doing well' has helped create an army of miserable obsessionals who never do anything because they are always striving for unattainable perfection. The tragic woman who polishes the bath fifty times, and still worries about whether or not it is really clean, is a result of this absurdly unrealistic expectation. Individuals who do manage to come to terms with reality, and recognise that 'done well and quick' is often more acceptable, more useful and more valuable than 'done perfectly and slowly' often spend their lives feeling guilty and frustrated. The truth is that everything in this life is a compromise between doing something well and doing it fast. Speed is often a more vital part of the equation than your parents seem to accept.

An obsessional surgeon who takes too long can be a threat to his patients. The longer an operation lasts the greater the risk of the patient dying on the operating table or suffering a complication afterwards. If, instead of spending a week on this column, I spent ten days writing it, then it would probably be over polished so much that it would read like a piece of bland nonsense from the Administrative Secretary at the Office of Loaves and Fishes. And in any case these pages would be blank because the column would never be delivered on time. It *has* to be written in seven days. Whether you are doing your homework, writing a book, painting a picture, making a movie or building a cupboard there has to come a time when you accept what you have done, stop and get on to the next job.

Your parents are right. If you spent five hours a night on your homework you'd probably eradicate the silly mistakes. And your marks might be better.

But you'd lose the ability to work quickly and under pressure (and so you would find examinations much harder). You would be constantly tired, jaded and bored and you would undoubtedly be less creative.

Your non scholarly interests will help make you mentally and physically fitter and stronger. If you let your parents decide the way you do your homework you'll probably come top of the class more often. But in five or ten years time no one will give a damn about who came top of your class. If you carry on the way you are then you'll be happier, healthier and much better equipped to deal with real life.

## PROGRESS

Why do politicians always talk about progress as if it was something good? In my experience when politicians, nationalised industries or big companies talk about progress what they really mean is that they are going to charge us more and provide a poorer service.

Since Stephenson invented the railways and Bell thought up the telephone, I have made train reservations by phone. A few days ago I had to travel to open an exhibition about the horrors of animal experiments. I telephoned the railway station and found myself listening to a pre-recorded message. So I telephoned another station. And then another. The man who eventually finished painting the booking office and picked up the receiver told me that I could no longer buy a ticket unless I turned up in person at an official sales point. It's got to be a round trip of at least 20 miles from where I live to any official sales point. This is what they seem to call progress and like you I don't care for it very much. The only answer is to write and complain about every bit of progress which you don't like. Don't leave it to everyone else because they're relying on you.

## CAN'T GET ENOUGH

My husband can't get enough sex. He says he gets pain in his testicles if he doesn't have sex at least two or three times a day. I am exhausted. We do it every morning and every evening—sometimes for two hours at a time—and my vagina is constantly sore. Once he made love to me six times in a row with hardly a break in between. Do you think he should see his doctor? I know this sounds odd but it has got to the stage where I would be happy if he'd find a mistress to take a bit of the pressure off me.

Yes, your husband should see his doctor. There could be a physical (and hopefully a soluble) explanation for his exhausting sexual appetite. Meanwhile, rather than finding him a mistress why not give your vagina a rest by providing him with manual relief?

## FLORIST

I want to start a business as a florist but my parents both say I'm too young and refuse to lend me the money. I am 26 years old. What do you think?

I don't think age has anything to do with it. Hannibal was Commander in Chief of the Carthaginian army at the age of 26—in charge of 40,000 troops and 38 elephants—so in that context running a florist's shop doesn't seem an entirely unreasonable ambition. At 26 you're old enough to screw up your own life. But by asking your parents to lend you the money you laid yourself wide open to getting their unwanted advice. It's a big, nasty world out there and the rules are simple: if you can gouge the loan you need out of a bank then you are old enough to start a business.

## REAL PIG

My boyfriend is a real pig. He treats me like dirt. He never asks my opinion and if I say anything he always sneers and makes me feel very small. I don't want to leave him because our sex life is terrific and he has a very large penis but how can I change him into a nicer person?

Your boyfriend sounds as if he is what he has—a large male organ. But since you stay with him because of the size of his penis you will, I hope, excuse me for pointing out that your relationship doesn't actually sound like the sort of love affair about which poets rhapsodise.

You can't and you won't change him (indeed it is always a mistake to begin a relationship in the belief that you will be able to change the person with whom you are beginning the relationship) so you will have to decide for yourself whether the downs of your relationship (being treated like dirt) outweigh the obvious ups.

............................................................

## SENSIBLE MAN

My husband is a very sensible person. He always keeps an old coat and a pair of rubber gloves in the car in case he has to change a tyre. He always has change in his pocket for car parks and tips. He always has a pen that works and if we're going somewhere by car he plans the route down to where we're going to stop for petrol, coffee and toilets. He always wears a pinafore and rubber gloves when he does the washing up and never makes a mess. We go shopping together on Saturday mornings. We make love on Saturday evenings and he always wears a condom even though I have been sterilised. We always make love in the missionary position and although he always comes first he always tries to give me an orgasm by using his fingers (for two years I've had to fake my orgasms simply because our love making is so predictable that I no longer find it exciting). On Sundays we clean the car and do the garden together.

In contrast to my husband I am totally disorganised and without him my life would, I know, be chaotic. I forget things, lose things and once got lost no more than five miles from home.

My husband is faithful and loyal and reliable but he is also dull, boring and predictable. I don't want to hurt him but the thought of spending the rest of my life in the rut he's built for us makes me want to scream. I would like to make love out of doors. I would love to have some adventure in my life.

Are you on probation and is your husband your probation officer? No? Well, stop whingeing then and start taking some responsibility for your own life. It's about time you started making a more positive contribution to the life you lead together. Take your husband by the rubber gloved hand and occasionally lead him astray and into temptation. For example, here's something you can try now.

Take off all your clothes and put on a coat or dressing gown. Then go and find your husband and, wherever he is and whatever he is doing, unfasten his trousers and kneel down in front of him. When you've got his penis in your mouth shrug off the coat you're wearing so that he can see that you're completely naked. If he's on the course at his golf club don't forget to wave through the players behind or else your husband could be in trouble with the committee.

If that sounds too adventurous for you then at least you'll now realise that you aren't quite the wild, unfettered free spirit you like to think you are!

Encourage your husband to let it all hang out occasionally. Persuade him to wear coloured socks that don't match his tie. Encourage him to accept crinkle cut chips instead of the straight edged ones. Talk him into staying in bed one Sunday morning and letting the car stay dirty for a whole week.

And here's a thought: how do you know that your husband isn't sensible and responsible because he thinks you want him to be sensible and responsible? Who knows, underneath those rubber gloves and that dainty little pinafore, maybe you could find a wild, tempestuous beast of a man just yearning to do unspeakable things to you in the local municipal park.

## JUST MISSED

Seven years ago I narrowly missed getting a job as a sales executive for a large, national company. Instead I got a job with a small family firm. The man who got the job I nearly got is now a very successful senior executive with the company. He earns a considerable amount more than I do, has two homes, two cars and a very enviable life style. I have recently discovered documentary evidence which shows that he lied about his qualifications on the application form for the job I so nearly got. What do you think would be the best way to go about making sure that his bosses get this information?

Do you think that if you get him fired you'll get the job you clearly think you ought to have got seven years ago? Or do you just want revenge for the fact that he has been more materially successful than you have? Either way you're allowing your envy to wreck your life. You are carrying around old resentments that are weighing you down, holding you back and souring your spirit. Why do you have to measure your life against his? And why must you keep on looking back when you would get so much more out of life if only you would look forward. There are setbacks and disappointments, narrow misses and 'almost made it' moments in everyone's life. But there are just as many new opportunities and fresh openings if you keep looking to the future. By concentrating on one professional disappointment and by allowing yourself to become embittered by what you clearly see as an injustice you have blinded yourself to fresh prospects.

Why not dump all this old shit. Bury it. Forget it. Burn your tawdry 'documentary evidence' as a symbol of your new determination to start enjoying the present and looking to the future instead of giving yourself (and probably becoming) a pain in the neck by constantly glancing over your shoulder at the past.

## VERY LONELY

I am very lonely. Every one else seems to have friends. Why can't I find friends? I really envy characters on TV programmes who always seem to be surrounded by friends.

You have to be a friend to have friends. And true friendships take time to mature. Like seeds growing in the garden you can't hurry friendships; you have to let them take root, you have to be patient and attentive. If you want long term friendships to flourish, you have to be prepared to put yourself out and you must accept the bad days as well as the good. To conquer your loneliness go to more places (pubs, clubs, evening classes) where you'll meet people. Strangers will slowly become acquaintances and from those acquaintanceships will be born friendships.

## AND FINALLY...

Don't slump down in front of the television set just yet because I have a present for you. It's a present that will not wear out or go out of fashion. It doesn't need batteries and you don't have to queue up to exchange it. It is a present that may make you feel uncomfortable for a few minutes but will, if you accept it, last for ever and change your life.

All I ask from you, in return for the gift I want to give you, is a little indulgence and a few moments of your time.

Of course, there is a chance you may not need my present. So, before we go any further let me ask you whether you think you have done as much as you can with your life. If you knew that you had just five minutes to live would you be satisfied that you had done as much as you could with your allotted lifespan?

If you aren't quite sure then read on.

Because I'm going to give you a philosophy for life.

Most people are dead at twenty five: their ambitions, hopes and aspirations confined to acquiring a car with 'genuine' vinyl seats and a fully paid up pension plan. They won't be buried for another half a century but they are doing little more than killing time until life runs out. They watch life drift by; never grasping their destiny or taking control. Thoreau was right when he wrote that 'the mass of men lead lives of quiet desperation'.

How many of your friends do jobs that they hate—and then excuse themselves by arguing that they need the money to pay for the stuff with which they have littered their lives? (And how much of that stuff—paid for with blood, sweat and tears—is worth the price that has been paid?)

How many people do you know who have sold their souls so that they can receive a pension in their old age? (And when you've suggested that they ought to have more fun how many times have you heard them say 'I'll have plenty of time and money to enjoy myself when I retire'?)

Don't let yourself be trapped in the same way.

And if you *are* trapped don't be afraid to break free.

You only get one chance at living. Don't sell your body, soul and mind so that you can buy an ice cream maker, a time share apartment in Marbella and a three piece suite in mushroom velour. Don't make the mistake of wasting your life on low expectations. Don't let your possessions own you and direct your life.

You may feel that you would like to do something with your life. But you may feel afraid. Dig down into your spirit and you will find dreams that just need dusting off.

Let your dreams out.

Why be afraid? What have you got to lose?

Take life by the scruff of the neck and shake it.

Whatever happens you will not regret the things which go wrong as much as you will regret the things you never do. Failing is no worse than not trying.

The saddest phrase in the English language is 'might have been'. When the game is over your regrets will tell you more about yourself than your accomplishments.

Don't make the mistake most people make—of worrying too much and thinking too little.

The secret of life is to be passionate.

If you do not dedicate your life to a cause about which you feel passionate you will eventually ask yourself whether life is worthwhile. And you will not know the answer.

Remember that the greatest irony of all is that you need something you are prepared to die for before you can get the most out of life.

With love and thanks for all your lovely letters.

Vernon Coleman

# PLAN 2000

EVERY 30 SECONDS 1000 animals die alone, frightened and in pain in laboratories.

- There are no laws requiring drug or cosmetic companies to perform animal experiments.
- Animal experiments are of no scientific or medical value: they are done because they help drug and cosmetic companies make money. Animal experiments are so misleading that they endanger human lives. Most drugs known to cause serious side effects when given to humans were originally tested on animals.
- Some of the animals tortured and killed in laboratories are family pets which have been taken off the streets. Others have been captured in the wild. The physical and mental suffering endured by these animals is incredible.
- Cats and kittens have their eyes sewn up while still alive.
- Chemicals are dropped into the eyes of live rabbits.
- Animals have chemicals injected directly into their brains—while they are still alive.
- Nearly three-quarters of the experiments are performed with no anaesthetic.

If you have a pet dog or cat and you want to know what vivisection really means, just imagine your pet friend stretched out on a vivisector's laboratory bench. Imagine the vivisector with scalpel poised. Imagine the look in the eyes of your *un*anaesthetised pet. And imagine the screams which follow.

If you *really* want to stop *all* animal experiments, join Plan 2000. For details please send a stamped, self-addressed envelope to:

**Plan 2000 Information Office**

234 Summergangs Road, Hull HU8 8LL, UK

*Also published by the European Medical Journal*

# Know Your Drugs
## Vernon Coleman

In addition to containing basic information—including side effects—about more than 100 of the most commonly prescribed prescription drugs, *Know Your Drugs* also includes:

- Tips for taking a prescription drug
- Common side effects
- How to read your prescription
- Ways to tell if your doctor is trying out a new drug on you
- Drugs which were so dangerous they had to be banned
- The top ten prescription groups
- Why you might have to take drugs for the rest of your life
- Questions to ask your doctor before taking a drug
- Drugs that are useless
- Tips for patients taking antibiotics
- Side effects which are common among elderly patients
- Why pregnant women should take care with drugs
- Tips for patients coming off tranquillisers
- Tips for women on the contraceptive pill
- Don't take pills indefinitely!

ISBN 0 9521492 5 7
160pp paperback

ALL ROYALTIES AND PROCEEDS GO TO HELP THE FIGHT AGAINST
ANIMAL EXPERIMENTATION.

Available from Book Sales, European Medical Journal,
Lynmouth, Devon EX35 6EE. Please write for a catalogue.

# Food for Thought
Your guide to healthy eating
Vernon Coleman

Packed with easy-to-use, up to date, practical information, *Food for Thought* is designed to help you differentiate between fact and fantasy when planning your diet. The book's 28 chapters include:

- Food the fuel: basic information about carbohydrates, protein, fat, vitamins and minerals
- When water isn't safe to drink—and what to do about it
- How what you eat affects your health
- Why snacking is good for you
- The mini-meal diet and the painless way to lose weight
- Quick tips for losing weight
- The Thirty-Nine Steps to Slenderness
- 20 magic superfoods that can improve your health
- The harm food additives can do
- 20-point plan for avoiding food poisoning
- Drugs and hormones in food
- Food irradiation, genetically altered food, microwaves
- 30 common diseases—and their relationship to what you eat
- How to eat a healthy diet
- 21 reasons for being a vegetarian
- How much should you weigh?
- How to deal with children who are overweight

ISBN  0 9521492 6 5  192pp  paperback

ALL ROYALTIES AND PROCEEDS GO TO HELP THE FIGHT AGAINST ANIMAL EXPERIMENTATION.

Available from Book Sales, European Medical Journal, Lynmouth, Devon EX35 6EE. Please write for a catalogue.

*Also published by the European Medical Journal*

# Betrayal of Trust
## Vernon Coleman

*Betrayal of Trust* follows in the tradition of Vernon Coleman's most iconoclastic and ground-breaking books—*The Medicine Men, Paper Doctors,* and *The Health Scandal.*

Dr Coleman catalogues the incompetence and dishonesty of the medical profession and the pharmaceutical industry and explains the historical background to the problems which exist today. He shows how drugs are put onto the market without being properly tested, and provides hard evidence for his astonishing assertion that doctors now do more harm than good.

To support his claim that drug companies use animal tests to get their drugs on the market, Dr Coleman lists scores of widely prescribed drugs which are reguarly prescribed for patients, despite the fact that there is evidence showing that the drugs cause serious problems when given to animals.

Drug companies are, he explains, in a 'no lose' situation. If a new drug seems safe when given to animals, the company making it uses that evidence to help get the drug a licence. But if a new drug causes problems when given to animals, that evidence is ignored as irrelevant! Only patients lose.

'When animal experiments are stopped,' says Dr Coleman, 'they will never be reintroduced. The moral, ethical, scientific and medical evidence all supports the contention than animal experiments must be stopped now.'

ISBN  0 9521492 2 2  160pp

ALL ROYALTIES AND PROCEEDS GO TO HELP THE FIGHT AGAINST ANIMAL EXPERIMENTATION.

Available from Book Sales, European Medical Journal, Lynmouth, Devon EX35 6EE. Please write for a catalogue.

*Also published by the European Medical Journal*

# How to Conquer Pain

A new and positive approach to the problem of
persistent and recurrent pain

## Vernon Coleman

A fully revised and updated edition of *Natural Pain Control.*
This book tells you
- Factors which influence the amount of pain you feel
- Doctors, drugs and pain control
- How to get the best out of pills
- Alternative therapies that work
- The unique Pain Control Progamme
- How to use your imagination to conquer your pain
- How to sleep when pain is the problem
- The magic of the TENS machine
- Learn how to relax and control your stress
- How to measure your pain
- •• and lots, lots more! ••

### *What they said about the first edition:*
☞ A clear and helpful handbook for pain sufferers… Perhaps
most important of all is the way in which it brings pain down
to a manageable level and gives self help ideas for sufferers.
*The Guardian*
☞ Full of good ideas  *Mother and Baby*
☞ A new and positive approach  *Keep Fit*
☞ An authoritative guide to this universal problem
*Bournemouth Evening Echo*

ISBN  0 9521492 9 X   192pp paperback

ALL ROYALTIES AND PROCEEDS GO TO HELP THE FIGHT AGAINST
ANIMAL EXPERIMENTATION.

Available from Book Sales, European Medical Journal,
Lynmouth, Devon EX35 6EE. Please write for a catalogue.

# Bodypower
## The secret of self-healing
### Vernon Coleman

*A new edition of a book that hit the Sunday Times and Bookseller 'Top Ten' charts*

- How your body can heal itself
- How your personality affects your health
- How to use bodypower to stay healthy
- How to stay slim for life
- How to conquer 90% of all illnesses without a doctor
- How to improve your eyesight
- How to fight cancer
- How to use bodypower to help you break bad habits
- How to relax your body and your mind
- How to use bodypower to improve your shape
- •• and much, much more! ••

*What they said about the first edition:*
☞ Don't miss it! Dr Coleman's theories could change your life
*Sunday Mirror*
☞ If you've got Bodypower, you may never need visit your doctor again, or take another pill! *Slimmer*
☞ A marvellously succint and simple account of how the body can heal itself without resort to drugs *Spectator*
☞ Could make stress a thing of the past *Woman's World*
☞ Shows you how to listen to your body *Woman's Own*
☞ Could help save the NHS from slow strangulation
*The Scotsman*

ISBN  0 9521492 8 1  192pp  paperback

ALL ROYALTIES AND PROCEEDS GO TO HELP THE FIGHT AGAINST ANIMAL EXPERIMENTATION.

Available from Book Sales, European Medical Journal, Lynmouth, Devon EX35 6EE. Please write for a catalogue.

# Mindpower

## How to use your mind to heal your body

### Vernon Coleman

*A new edition of this bestselling manual*

- A new approach to health care
- How your mind influences your body
- How to control destructive emotions
- How to deal with guilt
- How to harness positive emotions
- How daydreaming can relax your mind
- How to use your personal strengths
- How to conquer your weaknesses
- How to teach yourself mental self defence
- Specific advice to help you enjoy good health
- •• and much, much more! ••

### *What they said about the first edition:*

☞ Dr Coleman explains the importance of a patient's mental attitude in controlling and treating illness, and suggests some easy-to-learn techniques *Woman's World*

☞ An insight into the most powerful healing agent in the world—the power of the mind *Birmingham Post*

☞ Based on an inspiring message of hope *Western Morning News*

☞ It will be another bestseller *Nursing Times*

ISBN 1 898947 00 7   192pp   paperback

ALL ROYALTIES AND PROCEEDS GO TO HELP THE FIGHT AGAINST ANIMAL EXPERIMENTATION.

Available from Book Sales, European Medical Journal, Lynmouth, Devon EX35 6EE. Please write for a catalogue.

*Also published by the European Medical Journal*

# The Traditional Home Doctor

## Vernon Coleman

### *Packed with practical health tips*

Contents include:

- ANOREXIA - 7 tell-tale symptoms
- ARTHRITIS - 9 ways you can help yourself
- ASTHMA - 6 tips to help you cope
- BABY NOTES - 25 things to know about a newborn baby
- BACKACHE - 7 ways to avoid and 8 ways to conquer it
- CANCER - 10 ways to help fight cancer and win
- CHOKING - life-saving techniques
- COLDS AND FLU - 7 tips to help you stay healthy and 5 tips to help you fight colds and flu
- COT DEATH - 6 tips to keep your baby safe
- CRAMP - a simple remedy that works
- CRYING IN BABIES - 8 causes and the solutions
- DRY SKIN - 5 tips for making it feel soft again
- EMERGENCIES AND ACCIDENTS - practical advice
- FOOD - eating healthily
- HEADACHE - 3 ways of dealing with headaches
- HEART DISEASE - 8 tips to protect your heart
- HIGH BLOOD PRESSURE - 9 ways to keep it down
- HOME NURSING - 10 tips to help patient and nurse
- HYSTERECTOMY - 5 facts women should know
- INDIGESTION - 7 tips for sufferers
- IRRITABLE BOWEL SYNDROME - 4 solutions
- OVERWEIGHT - 18 tips to help you slim successfully
- PROSTATE GLAND - facts all men should know
- RELAXATION - how to relax your body and your mind
- SLEEPLESSNESS - 17 tips
- SNORING - 5 tips to help you stop it
- STRESS - 11 tips to help you conquer the stress in your life
- •• and much, much more! ••

ISBN 0 9521492 7 3  192pp

ALL ROYALTIES AND PROCEEDS GO TO HELP THE FIGHT AGAINST ANIMAL EXPERIMENTATION.

From Book Sales, European Medical Journal, Lynmouth, Devon EX35 6EE, UK.

*Please write for a catalogue.*